THE CHANGING FORMS OF IDENTITY POLITICS IN NIGERIA UNDER ECONOMIC ADJUSTMENT

The Case of the Oil Minorities Movement of the Niger Delta

Nordiska Afrikainstitutet
Uppsala 2001

This report was commissioned and produced under the auspices of the Nordic Africa Institute's programme "The Political and Social Context of Structural Adjustment in Sub-Saharan Africa". It is one of a series of reports published on the theme of structural adjustment and socio-economic change in contemporary Africa.

Programme Co-ordinator and Series Editor: Adebayo Olukoshi

Indexing terms
Structural adjustment
Ethnic groups
Minority groups
Petroleum industry
Nigeria
Niger Delta

Language checking: Elaine Almén

ISSN 1104-8425
ISBN 91-7106-471-0
© the author and Nordiska Afrikainstitutet 2001
Printed in Sweden by Elanders Digitaltryck AB, Göteborg 2001

Contents

Introduction 5

Contending Perspectives on Oil Minorities 9

Ethnicity, Ethnic Identity and Ethnic Minorities in the Niger Delta:
Some Conceptual Issues.. 12

Oil Minorities Identity Politics: A Historical Perspective 16

From Independence to the Outbreak of the Civil War................................ 20

The Nigerian Civil War and the Aftermath:
The Changing Fortunes of the Oil Minorities of the Niger Delta 24

Economic Crisis, Structural Adjustment and the Changing Forms
of Identity Politics of the Oil Minorities of the Niger Delta........................ 32

Structural Adjustment Programme in Nigeria:
Theoretical Foundations 39

The Impact of Structural Adjustment on Nigeria 42

Ethnic Identity Politics under Structural Adjustment................................. 48

The Changing Global and Domestic Environment 52

Oil Minorities Movements of the Niger Delta:
Patterns of Continuity and Transformation 68

New Trends, New Contradictions in the Delta:
Identity as National Liberation 71

The Globalisation of Local Struggles in the Niger Delta (1991–1999).......... 87

Decay and Renewal in the Oil Minorities Movements
of the Niger Delta.. 94

Trajectories of Ethnic Minority Politics in the Niger Delta:
Implications for the Nation-State Project in Nigeria 98

Concluding Remarks: Niger Delta Oil Minorities Movement
and the Future of Nigeria 102

References.. 108

Appendix 1. The Kaiama Declaration 118

Appendix 2. Ogoni Bill of Rights... 121

Appendix 3. Addendum to the Ogoni Bill of Rights.................................... 124

Introduction

This study explains the on-going transformations in ethnic minority identity politics in the oil producing parts of the Niger delta since the late 1980s. It also explores the linkages between structural adjustment and the decay and renewal, taking place within identity movements in the volatile oil-rich delta. The delta region had been noted for its struggles for self-determination since the second decade of the twentieth century (Tamuno, 1970; Saro-Wiwa, 1995), and has since been the site of ethnic minority struggles for a measure of autonomy during the period leading to independence in 1960. However, immediately after independence the struggles of these groups were limited to non-violent intra-elite or intra-class competition; or alliances with other ethnic minority groups making similar demands for their own states.

Recently, identity politics in the delta has become more pronounced, violent and widespread, even to the extent of threatening the Nigerian nation-state as presently constituted. The volatile nature of politics in the Niger delta, especially since the mid-1980s, is traceable to several factors: the emergence of petroleum as the fiscal basis of the Nigerian state, the status of petroleum as a critical element in the reproduction of the ruling class and the ultimate prize of political power. When it is considered that the bulk of the oil is extracted from the lands and waters of the Niger delta, it is not difficult to explain why the continued marginalisation of oil minorities of the delta from the centres of economic and political power has now become a volatile issue in Nigerian politics. This marginalisation derives from power relations characterised by the imposition by the Nigerian State of a centralised mode of access, extraction and distribution. It was further compounded by the deepening of economic crisis in the 1980s, a growing crisis of state legitimacy (Olukoshi, 1997: 452–460; Obi, 1997c), the intensification of authoritarian rule in a context of economic adjustment, and global changes attendant on the end of the cold war.

The foregoing combined to fuel the resurgence of ethnic movements and identity politics in the delta on an unprecedented scale and manner. Two decades of political exclusion from direct access to power and oil was interpreted in ethnic terms fuelling strong feelings among the "dispossessed" oil minorities that an end had to be put to the cheating. Identity thus became a marker of the quest for change, while itself undergoing transformation within the dialectics of the struggles for the "liberation" of the oil minorities from the hegemony of the dominant ethnic group factions and the oil multinationals operating in the delta. To capture the significance of these processes, it is necessary to examine the various forces, structures and modalities (and dynamics) through which the oil minorities movements are formed and transformed, and the roles played by extractive actors such as the Nigerian state and external economic/corporate interests (oil multinationals) in the on-going struggles.

The shrinking oil revenues accruing to the state as a result of the collapse of global oil markets in the late 1970s and 1980s, and the growing failure of the state to sustain the welfare gains of the immediate post-colonial and oil boom eras resulted in the deepening of contradictions within inter- and intra-ethnic relations. This crisis was worsened by the inability of structural adjustment to arrest economic decline, the intensification of economic extraction and the growing social hardship under the regime of free markets. The introduction of a two-party democracy in the early 1990s (under the rubric of a tightly controlled transition), under an environment of crisis and adjustment hardly helped matters. In the first place the transition excluded popular classes and all those opposed to adjustment, through the narrowing of the space for political participation (Ibrahim, 1993:129). This also meant that the grievances of the popular forces in the Niger delta had no platform or space in the political process; they decided to create their own autonomous space. Secondly, the struggle over shrinking oil rents in a context of a shrinking and militarised political space, severely undermined the "cement" binding class, state and nation in Nigeria. It was in this context that ethnicity gained more prominence as a tool of survival, mobilisation and the struggles to redefine power relations in society.

In response to the national crisis, ethnic identity movements began to reflect the widening of inter- and intra-ethnic and class cleavages, the redefinition of a collective "self" through the struggle for political space, and resources. The staking of claims to power and resources has grown, exhibiting a complex organisational capacity and striking power. The result has been the escalation of mistrust, tension and conflict, between those who control power, access and resources (and are unwilling to share or give up such power under any circumstances) and those to whom all access is blocked (who are made to bear the full cost of being powerless), with dire consequences for the fragile "homogenising" Nigerian nation-state project.

From the strong resurgence of identity politics in the Niger delta, it is possible to discern one of the most potent challenges to a Nigerian state that is clearly immersed in a legitimacy crisis. It strikes at the heart of the highly centralised hegemonic nation-state project being pursued by the ruling class in the following ways: by demanding that ethnic groups control their land and the resources found in their areas, insisting on the equality of all ethnic groups and the need for these groups to renegotiate the terms of their belonging to a Nigerian "nation", and most critical of all, insisting on a return to the derivation formula of revenue allocation in which national revenues would be shared proportionate to where they are derived from.

The economic crisis, the democratic struggles against military authoritarianism, as well as changes attendant to globalisation provided a fertile ground for the oil minorities to contest the stranglehold the elite factions of the majority (dominant) ethnic groups had over state (oil) power and access to fast shrinking resources. This historically determined pattern of majority ethnic group hegemony and its hegemonic nation-state project is being clearly confronted by the blocking power of the oil minorities who physically reside in (own) the oil producing region of Nigeria, and are in a position to literally cut off the lifeblood of the state. Beyond using their status as "oil landlords" to contest oil-power, and force a renegociation of their marginalised position within the Nigerian nation, the oil minorities are increasingly assuming the form of social movements operating within the ambience of popular power to pursue social justice, equity, environmental and political rights, which if successful, would radically transform the "unitary" Nigerian nation-state project. The struggles of the MOSOP, and the more recent agitation of the coalition of Ijaw (Ijo) movements which have pitched oil minorities against the federal government and oil multinationals aptly typify the volatile dynamics of identity politics in the delta.

While a lot has been written about the Ogoni (Loolo, 1981; Ngemutu-Roberts, 1994; Welch, 1995; Osaghae, 1995b; Boele, 1995; Crow, 1995; Naanen, 1995; Birnbaum, 1995; Cessou and Fatunde, 1995; Kretzman, 1995; Olukoshi, 1995; Cayford, 1996; CLO, 1996; Rowell, 1996; Saro-Wiwa, 1992, 1993, 1995; Robinson, 1997; Skogley, 1997; Ibeanu, 1997, 1999; Na' Allah, 1998; Obi, 1997a, 1998a, 1998b, 1999), the more recent travails of the Ijaw, the largest oil minority ethnic group are yet to be broadly captured. Yet, both exemplify the pattern of demands for restitution being ignored by the state and its "partners" the oil multinationals. Ultimatums for redress given by aggrieved oil minorities popular movements have been met by state repression, violence and extraction, thus feeding into a cycle of increasingly popular protests and resistance by these social movements which themselves express pent up rage and frustrations arising from the contradictions spawned in the local context by national and global forces (Obi, 1998a; Ihonvbere and Shaw, 1998: 224–225).

The transformation of these movements from ethnic minorities "in themselves" to ethnic minorities "for themselves" in the context of economic and political crises is a most critical element in the quest to deconstruct the unitary (apparently federal) nation-state project. As such, the military faction of the "national" ruling class using pretexts such as national security, unity, development, and the protection of strategic foreign investments and oil installations, has sought to crush ethnic (oil) minority resistance in the Niger delta by all and any means. The state (supported by the oil multinationals) has brutally repressed the uprisings in the delta, while showing a willingness to reward those indigenes of the delta who accept the hegemony of the extractive state-oil alliance. Their own people are increasingly branding such allies (indegenes) as sell outs or traitors. This trend reflects: the increasingly popular character of the oil minorities movement and the loss of legitimacy of the indigenous conservatives (pro-federal, pro-oil multinational) who are displaced by younger more radical elements. The popularisation of oil minorities movements have contributed to the expansion of demands to include the right to self-determination, control of resources and restitution for decades of expropriation and pollution. The change in the form, leadership and demands of the oil minorities movement are very significant as they touch on the very survival of Nigeria and the prospects for the resolution of the national-democratic crisis which entered a critical phase upon the annulment of the widely acclaimed free and fair presidential elections of June 1993 by the General Ibrahim Babangida-led military regime. For, without the resolution of the raging crisis in the delta in favour of the majority of the people, the prospects for enduring democracy in the Nigerian Fourth Republic expected to take off at the end of May 1999, could be bleak.

Contending Perspectives on Oil Minorities

The notion of oil minorities is a controversial and a rather complex one. While there is a broad agreement on the status of minority ethnic groups as those that are numerically small compared to others that are numerically preponderant, the concept of "oil minorities" has been hotly contested especially since the end of the civil war in 1970, when oil emerged as the fiscal basis of the Nigerian state. Thus, while ethnic groups such as the Hausa-Fulani, Igbo and Yoruba are considered the majority by virtue of their large demographic size (they allegedly account for roughly 60% of the populace), those like the Ijaw, Urhobo, Isoko, Andoni, Ogoni, Ndoni, Itsekiri, Kalabari, Ikwere, Ibibio, etc. (out of several hundreds of small groups) are referred to as ethnic minorities because of their smaller demographic size. Yet, some restraint needs to be exercised to avoid an oversimplification of the problem of minorities (Osaghae, 1998:2), or worse still, fetishize it. It is relevant that the notion of minorities be placed in political and social perspective. The tag of "oil" minorities evolved after the civil war, and gained prominence by the late 1980s as a modality of identifying those minorities, which, despite their connections to oil—the very lifeblood of Nigeria—have found themselves marginalised at the national level in terms of class, state and power.

The significance of demographic size lies in its connection with historical processes, social forces and political power. For the bigger ethnic groups with the head start they got under the colonial system of "indirect rule" and the sharing of spoils, have consolidated their access and control over power and resources in the post-colonial era. Furthermore, it set the scene for the subordination (and domination) of the minorities by the majorities within the context of inter- and intra-factional struggles for power. Inter-ethnic relations were therefore a highly politicised issue, determining to a large extent who got what, when and how much, and who controlled the coercive and extractive apparatuses of the state for private (personal), class or group gain. This meant that the executive of the state once captured by a hegemonic elite coalition or group could become an instrument of control and accumulation for the "victors" and exclusion and marginalisation for the "defeated". While the dominant groups favoured the centralised control of power (and resources), the minorities clamoured for decentralisation which would provide space for them to transcend the limitations of size in gaining access to power, and enjoying its benefits. To the ideologues of the "national unity project", minority agitation is inimical to stability and development, and by the same logic must not be allowed to "get out of hand", lest it "subverts" the march towards a homogenising project of the Nigerian nation-state.

In the zero-sum context of politics in an oil-dependent state, ethnicity plays a major role in defining the contending claims to oil. Those who claim the oil belongs to all Nigerians in the name of national unity, equal development and the national interest, reject the notion of oil minorities. They argue (citing relevant sections of the law to support this claim), that since the minorities of the delta did not put the oil in the ground, and do not tend the oil and gas the way you tend crops like cocoa, cattle or groundnuts, they cannot claim ownership of the oil, which "legally" belongs to the federal government and all Nigerians. Beyond this, some have cynically argued in the past, that the ethnic minorities of the Niger delta are too few to pose any serious threat to federal control of oil and "national" stability (Asiodu, 1980).

The counter-argument as put forward by the oil minorities is that since they have settled and lived on the land over the centuries, they own the land and everything in it (which includes the oil and gas). They also bear the full brunt of oil production: land expropriated for oil prospecting, exploration and extraction, and construction of oil installations and living quarters of oil company staff, degradation of the fragile delta environment by the activities of the oil industry, pollution of land and water bodies by oil spills, blowouts, gas flares and careless discharge/disposal of waste by the operating companies, government neglect, and widespread poverty, unemployment, and frustration. Furthermore, they posit that it is unjust for billions of dollars worth of oil to be extracted from a place, without anything being put back by the extractors in the form of development and welfare. The construction of the identity of oil minorities is a collective metaphor for their claims to the ownership of oil, their complaints of being unfairly treated and discriminated against because of their small size, and the injustice of their marginalisation from power in spite of the fact that they "own" (produce) the lifeblood of the Nigerian state. The analogy of the producers (land owners) being alienated from the products of their land (oil and gas) by the oil multinationals and the state, fits into the identity that the oil minorities have constructed in the quest for self-determination and liberation from their expropriators.

Despite the contestations around the concept of oil minorities, it can be argued that within the dialectics of Nigerian politics, the term aptly captures, not one, but an aggregation of small ethnic groups who share a commonality underlined by their physical location in the geography and political economy of oil, the lifeblood of the state, the very "glue" keeping the disparate groups, factions and elements that constitute Nigeria together. The opportunity cost of their hosting of a site of globally-led accumulation of oil capital, and the contradictions spawned in the locale further underscore the determinate role that oil has come to play in the lives of these people.

The concept of oil minorities is a very explosive and volatile one, mainly as a result of the high stakes of oil politics, the intersection of oil and state power, and the fear of the hegemonic faction of the Nigerian ruling class and its military allies that democracy will open up the political space to social forces that would break their monopoly over the providential oil wealth, or worse still, call them to account for the massive expropriation of millions of petro-dollars while Nigeria wallowed in debt and crisis. As such, the construction of an oil minority identity has other political connotations, apart from threatening the monopoly of the ruling class over oil. It also interrogates the logic of national unity, where there is inequity in the control and sharing of benefits from oil, thereby threatening the legitimacy of the homogenising nation-state project which guarantees the federal governments' control of oil. By the same token, it raises fears in the minds of the expropriators of the oil in the Niger delta over the possibility of secession, subversion, or a challenge to the homogenising nation-state project of the ruling class, or even worse, the disruption of oil operations in the Niger delta, which would gravely hurt the local interests of global oil capital and those of its local gatekeepers who have "privatised" the Nigerian state.

In the context of this paper, the concept of the oil minorities is clearly hinged on those minority ethnic groups who inhabit the Niger delta, host (or hosted) the oil multinationals and engage the state for restitution, the control of oil power, and the right to determine their own destiny as a people. Their fortunes as a people have become inextricably tied to the politics of oil. The global relations of oil have reshaped their very lives, robbing them of land, farmland, fishing grounds and livelihoods, and worse still forcing them to bear these heavy ecological and survival opportunity costs, while blocking the path to restitution and redress. Issues of exclusion, marginalisation and inclusion in the power relations spawned by oil, pitch the oil minorities against those with power over oil. The state, which mediates relations between global oil and the people of the oil-producing communities, becomes both a site of the struggle, and a critical player in the politics of oil. Oil minority as an identity becomes a counter-claim to those of the hegemonic groups who dominate the state. In this push and pull of forces, the balance of power within and between the contending groups, locally and globally, determines the outcome. A key issue in the local or national context is the "question of centralised versus distributed power" (Cayford, 1996:186), within the ambience of ethnic majority–oil minority relations, as mediated by the Nigerian state.

Yet, there is an acknowledgement that the politics of the oil minorities can be complex, fluid and contingent upon calculations of gain by the various contending forces and groups. It reflects internal cleavages, internal contradictions, cross ethnic intra-class alliances, which also show that the oil minorities movements are still defining and redefining themselves through their struggles against the combined might of the Nigerian state and oil multinationals.

Ethnicity, Ethnic Identity and Ethnic Minorities in the Niger Delta: Some Conceptual Issues

A critical step towards analysing ethnic identity politics is the notion of ethnicity, its evolution in the context of Nigeria's politics, and its resurgence in a period of economic and political crisis. A lot has been written on ethnicity or ethnic politics in Nigeria (Anifowose, 1982; Nnoli, 1978, 1994, 1995; Otite, 1990; Ihonvbere, 1994; Osaghae, 1991, 1995a, 1995b, 1996, 1998; Adekanye, 1995; Soremekun and Obi, 1993b; Saro-Wiwa, 1989, 1992, 1994b). Equal attention has also been paid to ethnic minority politics (Osaghae, 1991, 1995a, 1996, 1998; Okpu, 1977; Allagoa and Tamuno, 1989; Akinyele, 1990; Ihonvbere and Shaw, 1998; Suberu, 1993, 1996; Udogu, 1994, 1997; Obi, 1995, 1997a, 1998b, 1998d).

At the conceptual level, there has been a discernible shift from the debates between those who viewed ethnicity as a paradigm for explaining politics in Africa, and those who viewed it as a disruptive or negative element which had to be transcended in any accurate analysis of African politics (Doornbos, 1998; Obi, 1998a). The reasons for the renewed interest in ethnicity perhaps lies in its "resilience", but more in its resurgence as a potent force "following the changed political conditions in Africa in the wake of structural adjustment and its repercussions" (Doornbos, 1998:17). This development is also partly due to the following: increased pressures within Africa for democracy, the return to multi-partyism, economic crisis, a global climate supportive of democracy, civil rights and minority rights, declining legitimacy of the postcolonial state, and pressures for the decentralisation or democratisation of the state (Doornbos, 1998; Laakso and Olukoshi, 1996:7–8). A major concern is how ethnicity will express itself or "take advantage" of the changing environment, and the implications of the transformation of ethnic identity for the nation-state project in Africa.

At this point, it is important to deal with the question of ethnicity and interrogate certain assumptions. Osaghae (1995b:11) defines the phenomenon of ethnicity as "the employment and or mobilisation of ethnic identity or difference to gain advantage in situations of competition, conflict or co-operation". The ethnic group is therefore one, "whose members share a common identity and affinity based on a common language and culture, myth of common origin and a territorial homeland, which has become the basis for differentiating "us" from "them", and upon which people act". In a more recent study, Osaghae (1998:3) argues that "minorities in Nigeria may be defined in contradistinction to the three major ethnic groups in the country—Hausa-Fulani, Yoruba and Igbo—as linguistically, culturally, territorially and historically distinct groups which have been subjected to subordinate political, social and economic positions in the federation and its constituent units". According to

Nnoli, "ethnicity arises when relations between ethnic groups are competitive rather than co-operative. It is characterised by cultural prejudice, and political discrimination" (Nnoli, 1995:1). Ethnic identity following this logic is the instrumentality through which the ethnic group "plays" politics. Identity is thus the political key to the engine room of ethnicity as a mobilising element for the capture of power. Ethnicity need not at all times be a game of numbers, for it is possible for smaller ethnic groups through a combination of historical (and socio-economic) factors and mobilisational capacities and by their position in a given structure of power relations to dominate larger groups (Osaghae, 1998: 3; Oyediran, 1996). As a political phenomenon, it occupies a critical place at the intersections of class, state and power (Doornbos, 1998:19). Its significance can be further captured through a concrete analysis of the balance of forces within a given social formation and their connections with the state and the global capitalist system.

It is important to caution against a static notion of ethnic identity. Ethnic groups should not be treated as homogenous ethnic wholes. They are dynamic, continuously being constructed and transformed socially, and have cleavages along the lines of class, ideology, history, and politics, and even personality differences cannot be discounted. Ethnic groups can also be transformed by a combination of factors as discussed earlier. They can enter into alliances with classes in other ethnic groups, or an individual (or a small clique) can mask his or her personal or narrow interests as those of an ethnic group or coalition, depending on power and influence, and a benefit-cost analysis. Without being drawn into the debate of the positive or negative aspects of ethnicity, the real issues become how state-society relations are mediated through ethnicity, the nature of the ethnicity-economics interface, how ethnic identity politics finds expression in state-civil society relations, and the implications of the foregoing for the nation-state project in Nigeria in a rapidly globalising world.

The resurgence of ethnicity can be defined within the power relations corresponding to the nature of the re-invigorated drive by global neo-liberal forces to integrate Nigeria further into the international capitalist system. Ethnic identity is thus transformed into a mobilising element not only for contesting access to state and oil power within a context of competing and conflicting ethnicity, but also a modality for organising social forces to resist alienation, extraction and exclusion by the hegemonic coalition of the ethnic elite. Beyond the usual thesis of competing ethnicities seeking access to power, patronage and resources, oil minorities politics reflect the changing forms of inter-class, intra-ethnic relations and strategies through which the popular classes (radical elite, youth, student, women, peasant, and professional groups), are contesting the leadership of these movements, and pushing a counter-hegemonic nation-state agenda that seeks to deconstruct the currently centralised, authoritarian and crisis-ridden one.

At another level, ethnic identity politics are partly a response to global trends. An important point is the location of the oil-rich ecology of the Niger delta in globalised oil relations. On the one hand, the Nigerian state mediates the relations between the global and the local, facilitating the extraction of oil and accumulation of oil capital. While on the other, the global is domesticated in the Niger delta, exercising power, playing politics, extracting oil, degrading the ecosystem and alienating the "oil landlords" from the products of their lands and waters. Identity politics respond both to the changing global environment and intensified extraction of oil under adjustment by adopting a global platform of minority rights to resist globalised oil expropriation. The identity of the "victim", an indigenous people being violated by western corporate oil interests is mobilised both locally and globally to challenge the state and oil multinationals. In this way, the social movements of the delta adopt an agenda of national liberation (self-determination), civic and environmental rights and democracy. Perhaps, the most successful of such movements in the Niger delta has been the Movement for the Survival of Ogoni People (MOSOP) which confronted the Nigerian state and Shell, and internationalised its struggle for self-determination, social justice and an end to expropriation by global oil capital from 1990.

The ethnicity-economics interface finds expression in the nexus between economic adjustment and the upsurge in ethnicity in Nigeria (Adekanye, 1995; Osaghae, 1995; Laakso and Olukoshi, 1996). This interface is often acute as a result of the relative poverty of the Nigerian elite, leading it to depend on the state and on foreign capital for accumulation purposes. As a lot of premium is placed on gaining access to lucrative niches in the political economy, ethnicity becomes yet another instrument in the quest of the elite to organise for the capture of resources. In a context of economic crisis where less oil revenues flow into the states coffers, scarcities, distributive inequities build up and feed into more intense struggles over shrinking resources. These are further compounded by the rolling back of the welfare frontiers of the state through adjustment; contradictions between and within ethnic groups deepen, fuelling more mistrust, conflict and violence. In order to contain these struggles, and blunt the edge of class struggles from below, the state has relied on authoritarianism, both as a modality of defending oil-based accumulation and forcing through its homogenising nation-state project which guarantees it the monopoly of control over the oil-fields in the Niger delta.

Without doubt, part of the crisis besetting the nation-state in Africa is the fall-out of the homogenising process of the post-colonial state project (Laakso and Olukoshi, 1996:9). In Nigeria this homogenising process has been problematic and is currently being undermined by authoritarianism, socio-economic crisis, and the inequities embedded in the distribution of power in an ethnically plural oil rentier context. These pressures have not only contributed to the resurgence of ethnicity, but have laced it with violence and conflict. What is particularly interesting is that the construction of, and content of the demands of ethnic identities, as in the case of oil minorities, under crisis and adjustment, reflect popular and democratic aspirations. This implies that the current crisis and ethnic (oil) minority identity politics can dialectically feed into, and enrich a democratic and sustainable nation-state project in Nigeria. The challenge is to capture the possibilities the paroxysms of ethnic identity politics can help provoke on a broader scale a process that will lead to an equitable and democratic basis for the resolution of the national question.

Oil Minorities Identity Politics: A Historical Perspective

The treatment of the identity politics of the oil minorities of the Niger delta can be divided into several phases to capture its development: the origins and evolution up till the outbreak of the Nigerian civil war in July 1967, the ascendancy and changes from the outbreak of the war till the coming to power of the Babangida regime through the 1985 coup, and since the onset of adjustment in the later half of the 1980s. This enhances an understanding of the elements and changes in the dynamics of the minorities movement of the delta. An important point is the relationship between identity politics and state power, and the position of oil minorities in the "national" division of labour, which itself has remained an appendage of globally led accumulation of capital.

Origins and Evolution

Ethnic minorities are a creation of the Nigerian colonial state. It is tied to the forceful bringing together of various people, economies and polities by Britain, and defining them territorially as Nigerians. Although these "minorities", before colonialism had some relations through trade, diplomacy and war, with their neighbours, as well as the European traders that came calling at the coast, they were largely autonomous city-states and Kingdoms. It was the territorial definition of Nigeria that subordinated them as a numerically small constituency within an outpost of British imperialism. "Ethnic minorities" were also the product of the intersection of ethnicity with class as spawned by the relations of power arising from colonial capitalism. Although the colonial state theoretically treated all the ethnic groups as "equals", the reality of colonial patrimonialism, the "divide and rule" structure of colonial governance and the emergence of an intermediary Nigerian class to facilitate extraction and maintain order tended to give the advantage to the elite from the numerically dominant groups. It also created schisms and inequalities between and within the groups. As noted elsewhere (Obi, 1998b:263):

> Essentially, the Nigerian colonial state served the interests of global accumulation in the periphery through the local extraction and transfer of resources to the metropolis. As such it exacerbated local differences and spawned uneven development through vertical channels of extraction, accumulation and transfer. Uneven levels of penetration, regional disparities in the emergence of the local elite in areas of concentration of accumulation and commerce (to the detriment of those excluded), created cleavages, distrust and rivalry.

When it became clear to this elite after the Second World War that it would inherit political office once the colonialists left Nigeria, ethnic identity became a critical modality for legitimacy and organising mass support to capture power. Those who had the natural advantage of numbers and occupied a critical position in the colonial structure of governance and the accumulation of capital (from the export of cash crops, tin, columbite and coal), were able to organise for the capture of power to the exclusion of "the few". Accordingly, "it was the ethnic nationalism instigated by the elite in majority groups, more than the lumping together of unequal groups, that brought about the problem of minorities" (Osaghae, 1991:239). Minorities were defined in the Nigerian context by the intersection of size and power, and the dynamics of the class formation project spawned by colonial capitalism. The elite from all groups deployed "politicised ethnicity" in the quest for space and power; it was however those favoured by the colonial system, size and organisational capacities that pressed home their advantage.

The Nigerian ruling elite nurtured in the womb of the colonial state—an artificial structure functioning for the accumulation of capital—was divided, reinforcing competition in ways that reflected their exclusion from accumulation, but betrayed a desire to be recognised as "junior partners", depending on the influence they could wield in the territory defined for them by the colonial state. Appeals to ethnic symbols, solidarity and the realisation of collective greatness based on myths of a common origin and destiny, sometimes festooned with religion, were used and manipulated by "elite nationalists", who lacked a strong economic base, and saw the advantage of building "nationalist" alliances with the popular classes to organise for the capture of power and office. From the onset, this nationalist elite had no quarrel with capital, the problem was how to organise to capture power, and use the state as a platform to accumulate capital. Ethnicity was a tool of the elite both for competing and co-operating for the capture of power, and for dividing the masses of the people that had begun to protest the inequities of colonial capitalism. Vertical ethnic linkages sought to block horizontal linkages between the popular classes across the country, by asking the people to queue behind "ethnic nationalists" in the competition for resources and welfare, and much later, in the quest for Nigeria's independence.

According to Okpu (1977), "ethnic nationalities did not become a part of the vocabulary of Nigeria until after the regionalisation was begun in the mid-1940s". This same claim resonates in most of the literature on the ethnic minority question in Nigeria. It is hinged upon the fact that the division of Nigeria into three (unequal) administrative regions by the British (through the Richards constitution) roughly coincided with the "territory" of the three ethnic majorities: Hausa-Fulani (Northern region), Yoruba (Western region) and the Igbo (Eastern region) thus providing a tripod for polarising Nigerians along the lines of ethnicity.

The North, the biggest of the three regions was larger than the East and West combined. This laid the foundation for its having a preponderance of representation and power over the other regions at the federal level. To protect themselves and their economic base from their counterparts in the North, the bourgeoisie of the West and East worked towards a federation founded on strong regions and a weak centre. Furthermore, the fact that each of the majority ethnic groups was numerically dominant in each region led to the creation of ethnic minorities in each of the regions. These were located in the Midwest, Calabar-Ogoja-Rivers area in the South, and the Middle-Belt, Southern Zaria, and Borno in the North. Thus emerged competition at two levels: between the ethnic majorities, and between each ethnic majority and the ethnic minorities. In the Eastern region, the minorities reinforced their age-old quest for self-determination and freedom from Igbo hegemony. The Ijaw Peoples Congress (IPC), formed in 1941 to agitate for the creation of the Rivers Province out of the Owerri Province succeeded, when the Rivers Province was created in 1947 (Naanen, 1989).

Like their counterparts in the other regions, the minorities saw in "politicised ethnicity" a major asset for organising themselves to gain access to power at the regional and federal levels. Majority-minority relations were broadly super-ordinate-subordinate relations, but ethnicity mediated through the state later produced some significant exceptions either through minorities' elite in one region aligning with majorities (or a dominant party) in another, with themselves, or taking advantage of special relationships fostered within the pre-colonial and colonial political economy to become influential minorities. Worthy of mention are some coastal people (for example the Itsekiri, Ijaw and Efik) who had been involved in four centuries of Trans-Atlantic trade, and had built up commercial and social links and influence with which they were able to dominate their neighbours especially those in the hinterland.

From the late 1940s particularly after the Macpherson constitution of 1951, which laid a federal basis for the nationhood of an ethnically plural Nigeria, on the basis of unity in diversity, all the groups started to organise for power. Ethnic nationalism and ethnicity involving majority groups rotated around elite or aristocratic-led cultural organisations: Jamiyya Mutanen Arewa-Northern Region, Egbe Omo Oduduwa-Yoruba, and the Igbo State Union-Igbo. These groups were based on ethnic identity and formed the nucleus of the political fighting machine of an elite eager to inherit the colonial state. Jamiyya, evolved into the Northern Peoples Congress (NPC), Egbe, into the Action Group (AG), while the Igbo Union formed a hegemonic bloc within the (Pan Africanist, later Pan-Nigerian) National Council of Nigerian Citizens (NCNC). When Nigeria embarked on regional self-rule in1954 the NPC, AG, and the NCNC swept the polls and dominated power in their respective regions. Some of the minorities transformed their own cultural organisations into political parties, but these did not feature much until they evolved into states' creation movements in the early 1950s (see Table 1).

The minorities were marginalised in the regions, both in terms of participation in the structures of governance, distribution of public and elective offices, and access to resources and services. As such, the elite and people of the minorities' areas were disadvantaged in the structure of class relations prevalent shortly before independence. Suffocated within the class and ethnic politics of their regions, they sought allies amongst minorities in their regions

Table 1. *Main Ethnic Minority Movements in the Niger delta in the 1950s*

Calabar-Ogoja-Rivers State Movement
Midwest State Movement
Niger Delta Congress

Source: Ugbana Okpu, *Ethnic Minority Problems in Nigerian Politics: 1960–1965*. Uppsala: Studia Historica Upsaliensia, 1977.

and majorities in other regions. This it was hoped would provide some leverage against regional hegemonists in their own regions to make some concessions to the elite of the minorities who had mobilised their own people for the capture of power. According to Osaghae (1991), as independence became imminent, the minorities supported the opposition party in their regions: in the North, the United Middle-Belt Congress aligned at different times with the AG and the NCNC, in the West, the Midwest State Movement aligned with the NCNC, while the COR Movement supported the AG. Minorities movements evolved into states' creation movements, in which the elite sought exclusive space to accumulate, reproduce itself and gain a platform for staking claims and gaining access to power at the federal level. Of immediate relevance is the cross ethnic minority coalition, the Calabar-Ogoja-Rivers Movement that sought the creation of states for minorities in the south-east and delta areas of Nigeria. Tamuno (1970), re-calls that the Rivers state movement had its roots in the 1940s based on the discrimination it suffered under Igbo hegemony in the Eastern region. This movement later metamorphosed into the Niger Delta Congress under the leadership of Dappa-Biriye in 1953 (Naanen, 1989). Pressures on the colonial government to create states contributed to the setting up of the Willink Commission to Enquire into the Fears of Minorities and the Means of Allaying Them, in 1957. Beyond the insertion of some constitutional guarantees and the setting up of a board for the development of the Niger delta; the recognition of the peculiar needs of the delta minorities and the deprivations they suffered did not translate into the creation of states nor any developmental effort until well after independence in 1967. Thus, between 1960 and 1967, the elite of the delta either formed pressure groups or entered coalitions which continued with the demands for states of their own, or joined in the struggle for power at the regional and federal levels where their chances of success were slim, and the available openings, very few, and of little political weight.

From Independence to the Outbreak of the Civil War

At independence in 1960, identity politics in the Niger delta, though the demands for space and direct access to resources had been blocked by the ethnic hegemonists who controlled power in the regions and their partners in the "metropole", built alliances with opposition parties in each region. This however attracted reprisals from the ruling party in the region. It was however only in the case of the Midwest region, that a state was created for the ethnic minorities of the Western region. In some way, it was the outcome of the collusion between the NPC-NCNC alliance against the opposition party, AG, which held sway in the Western region, and was the party in opposition at the federal level. For while the parties gave support to state creation movements outside their spheres of influence, they resisted any attempt to create states in their own exclusive "fiefs"—the regions.

The issue of the mode of integration of Nigeria into global capitalism and the sharing of surplus from peasant-based agriculture featured prominently in intra-class and inter-class relations mediated through ethnicity. The so-called revenue allocation was an important source of surplus for class formation and reproduction. The dominant principle of revenue allocation at this time was derivation, which allocated the bulk of revenues accruing to government to the regions from which they were derived (got). In this way, the elite from the majority ethnic groups cornered the cash crop economic base of each region. When this base began to collapse in the wake of the fall in global prices and demand for cash crops, a problem arose both for the regional elite, and the terms of their participation in the nation-state project. The fact that the cash crop base was to be replaced by petroleum from the minorities' area of the Eastern region, meant that a new struggle would ensue over oil. As Pearson (1970) put it:

> ... in 1965, the Federal Prime Minister in a statement to the Chamber of Commerce ... spoke optimistically about the balance of payments impact that oil production would have in Nigeria. Politically, feelings about petroleum ran high. Interest in controlling oil grew.

Several developments influenced the politics of the ethnic minorities of the Niger delta: continued marginalisation from regional power, zero-sum competition between the regional power-elite, the determination of the NPC-led federal government to crush the opposition, and the collapse of world prices for cash crops alongside the significance of growing petroleum exports from the Niger delta by the mid-1960s. According to Rimmer (1978:149), "while agricultural exports declined by 40 per cent between 1964 and 1974, the volume of oil exports increased by more than fivefold between the same times". Although a few members of the minorities' elite sought and gained entry into the regional and federal levels of governance, they hardly made any impact in their ethnic/class constituencies, and in real terms occupied subordinate positions in the national ruling class coalition. Most of the minorities' elite continued to meet and organise for the creation of states as a modality of creating an exclusive space for accumulation, and bargaining for access for power at the centre. For them, inter-majority group (regional) rivalry and the growing significance of oil exports could be exploited to provide leverage to their demands for states. This knowledge was also not lost on the other factions of the Nigerian ruling class who now turned their attention to the new wealth of the Nigerian nation, oil. The control of oil had become critical to the struggle for power. As Beckman (1981) notes:

> It was only by the mid-1960s that the production of oil began to have a notable impact on public finance. The question of the control over oil producing territory (mainly the delta of the Niger river and the continental shelf) and the method of dividing the revenue were crucial in the ongoing struggles between centralising and separatist tendencies.

Now the regional basis of accumulation had shifted from the regions (West-cocoa, North-groundnuts, hides and skin, and East-palm produce), to the Niger delta-petroleum, the zero-sum struggle raged around what configuration or elite coalition would organise to capture power over oil. For while the existing regional structure and derivation would favour the Igbo elite control of oil, and give them the leverage to dictate terms, it would not confer the same access or powers on the others.

According to some sources, the Northern Nigerian bourgeoisie had warned their Eastern counterparts in 1965 against staking such claims to the oil in the Niger delta (Ikein and Briggs-Anigboh, 1998:103). Since the oil was in the Igbo-dominated Eastern region, the elite from the two majority groups (Hausa-Fulani and Yoruba and the minorities in the Eastern region (Niger delta), had a common interest in resisting Eastern claims to the oil. This found expression in a national unity project constructed after the coups of 1966 in January and July, and shortly before the outbreak of the civil war in July 1967, when the Igbo made good their threat to pull the Eastern region out of the Nigerian federation. But before this, there had been an attempt by a small group of Ijaw activists (the Niger Delta Volunteer Force) led by Isaac Adaka Boro (a former University of Nigeria undergraduate and ex-policeman), Sam Owonaro and Nottingham Dick, to secede from Nigeria through force of arms by proclaiming the Niger Delta Republic in February 1966. They launched an attack from their base in Yenagoa in the heartland of Ijaw territory on a police station and some government offices on February 24, 1966 (Okpu, 1977:136; Kaemi, 1982). Their short-lived "twelve day revolution" was based on the desire to end the marginalisation of the delta minorities, the suspicion that Ironsi government would seize the oil resources of the Niger delta, and a determination to assert Ijaw control of oil.

The Boro-led revolt was however crushed by federal troops after surrounding Kaiama, Boro's birthplace, ending in the arrest, trial and the sentencing of the "revolutionaries" to death after being found guilty of committing treason. Before the sentences could be carried out, Gowon had seized power through the counter-coup of July 1966. He granted them pardon and they were released. Adaka joined the Nigerian army and fought on the federal side during the civil war. He later lost his life at the war front during the effort to push out the Biafran rebels from the Niger delta.

The ethnic interpretation given to the coups (the first as an Igbo attempt to dominate Nigeria, and the second as a Northern response) deepened the contradictions within the Nigerian ruling class. Ethnic identity, particularly that of the minorities of the Niger delta gained unprecedented political importance as allies that could tilt the balance either way: in favour of the centralising or separatist tendencies in the federation, as those who "possessed" the emergent economic base of Nigeria, oil. The struggles around oil raised the premium on oil minorities as strategic allies, without whom no one could corner the potentially immense oil wealth.

In 1966, a delegation of Rivers Leaders of Thought, presented a memorandum demanding the creation of Rivers state to the military head of state, Colonel Yakubu Gowon, demonstrating a belief that succour could only come from the federal side, and expecting it to recognise the benefit of dealing fairly with the oil minorities. The northern elite which had considered the succession option after the 1966 crisis, came round to accepting that with the reality of a shrinking regional cash crop and tin export base, oil, located far away in the delta would be the best viable option for continued participation in national and global accumulation. It was therefore in its interest to remain a part of the Nigerian nation-state project as a guarantee of unbridled access to oil. In the new strategic calculus of the northern regional elite, buoyed no doubt by the advice and interests of its local as well as western friends, the time had come to court the oil minorities—the gateway to the vast, virtually limitless oil wealth of the Niger delta.

The oil minorities became the new "Cinderella" of ethnic identity politics in Nigeria, and by May 1967, they had won two states, Rivers and the Southeastern state to the bargain, thus satisfying to an extent the age-old demand of the elite for an exclusive political and economic base. The minorities' faction thought that now they had their own "states", they had exclusive claim to and control of the oil wealth of their region. To them, it was a sign of the success of their struggles for self-determination since the early part of the century, and the prospects were that with the new found economic power, they would have more leverage over the majority ethnic groups. It was a calculation that turned out to be wrong by the time the Nigerian civil war ended in 1970 (Saro-Wiwa, 1989). The nationalist coalition that fought and won the Nigerian civil war did so under the banner of a national unity project. This meant several things: the supremacy of the national over the sectional, the centralisation of control over economic and political power as a means of preventing the sectional or regional from becoming strong enough to challenge or threaten the federal government, and the ascendancy of a homogenising ideology of the Nigerian nation-state, no doubt buoyed by an oil-boom induced confidence.

The Nigerian Civil War and the Aftermath: The Changing Fortunes of the Oil Minorities of the Niger Delta

The reasons for the outbreak of the Nigerian civil war are well known and will not be repeated here. What is important is the involvement of the oil minorities in this war, and how it influenced their politics. In the months leading up to the war two significant developments had taken place: northern officers had led the overthrow of the regime of an Igbo officer, General J.T.U. Aguiyi-Ironsi (who had taken over power after the botched coup of January 15, 1966 in which the federal Prime Minister, the Premier of the Northern region, and some senior officers of northern origin had been killed) which had imposed a unitary system on the country, and Colonel Odumegwu Ojukwu, the governor of the Eastern region had made good his threat to pull his region out of the Nigerian federation (after organised pogroms against Igbo people living in the northern region and disagreements with Gowon over the interpretation of the Aburi Accord on what political structure Nigeria should adopt), by declaring it the republic of Biafra.

One of the earliest actions Ojukwu took after the proclamation of Biafra was to instruct oil multinationals operating in the Niger delta on June 4, 1967 to "pay rents, royalties, and other affiliates to his government" (Ikein and Briggs-Anigboh, 1998:128). By this action he concretised the claims of the regional elite to the oil in the Niger delta, and incidentally provided a basis for the unity of elite from the other regions and the minorities to contest such claims. The federal government replied by warning the oil multinationals against making any such payments to Ojukwu. The separatist and decentralising tendencies of Ojukwu's Biafra clashed with the national unity and centralist position of the federal government, especially as it related to the contestation over oil. The creation of twelve states out the old four region structure on May 27, 1967 by Colonel Yakubu Gowon the Nigerian military head of state, literally took the wind out of the sails of the Igbo bourgeoisie, by creating two states out of the minorities area of the Niger delta, thus creating space for their elite to operate. They also gained some representation at the federal level.

The new offices created and the fresh appointments made provided the oil minorities' elite with an economic and political base, while the masses, who had all the time aligned with the elite hoped that now they had got their own states, their lives would improve considerably. The balance in the delta quickly tilted in favour of a federal project that provided exclusive space for the oil minorities' elite in the governments of Rivers and South-Eastern state. As such, most of them supported the federal government in wresting their oil-rich land from Biafra. This is not to deny the role of some individuals who supported Biafra, but these were few in number, and had little following in the delta.

Thus, the oil minority elite featured prominently in the military and political effort to defeat Biafra. Its support for the federal unity project was a tactical move calculated to overthrow the oppressive Igbo domination, stave off Igbo claims to oil, and provide access to surplus and wealth within newly defined fiefs. In July 1967, the federal navy imposed a blockade on Bonny and Port Harcourt oil export terminals, after warning the oil multinationals against making any payments to Biafra (Cronje 1972; Turner, 1978). At the same time, the federal army entered into the region to end the secession. When Bonny (a strategic island in the delta hosting an oil export terminal) was liberated, Ken Saro-Wiwa, a twenty six year old of ethnic minority origin, and an Ogoni activist (and ex-assistant lecturer at the University of Nigeria, Nsukka) involved in the movement for the creation of Rivers state, was appointed the administrator of Bonny by the federal government. He was after the war appointed as a commissioner in the executive council of the Rivers state government (which was manned by indigenes of the state), a position from which he was to be sacked in 1973. During and after the war, politicised ethnicity had helped the elite of the Niger delta gain access to the state, and the increased significance of oil also brightened their prospects for a huge chunk of the oil surplus. Osaghae (1998:11) vividly captures the changed fortunes of the minorities in Nigeria:

> With the abrogation of the problematic regions and the creation of twelve states in 1967, partly to ensure their support, minorities emerged from the war as a more vocal and assertive group, conscious of their role in the federation.

Even if the minorities of the oil-rich Niger delta emerged as a more assertive group at the end of the Nigerian civil war, they had not won the power over "their" oil. Neither did they enjoy the same privileges and influence as the northern minorities who had played a very prominent role in the military effort to stabilise the Nigerian state. This can be traced to the following: the transfer of the military command structure to the federal-state government relations, effectively subordinating the latter to the former, the strategic role played by some officers of northern minority origin in the 1966 counter-coup and the execution of the war by the victorious federal army. Other factors included: the centralisation of the collection of all oil revenues in the federal government, the vesting of all ownership and right to produce oil in the federal military government, and the de-emphasis on derivation as a sole principle of revenue allocation in favour of population and the equality of states. Yet, to differentiate themselves from other minorities, and underscore their strategic position vis à vis oil, the minorities of the Niger delta took on the identity of "oil" minorities. This identity has become a critical label in the politics of national-building in Nigeria ever since.

Federal control of oil was legitimised by decree No. 51 of 1969, which:

> ...vested in the federal military government the entire ownership and control of all petroleum: in, under or upon any lands in Nigeria; under the territorial wa-

ters of Nigeria (note increase in Nigerian territorial waters by decree No. 38 of 1971 to 30 miles); or all land forming part of the continental shelf of Nigeria (Etikerentse, 1976, 1985).

In addition to the proceeding, Section 2 of the decree gave the federal commissioner of Mines and Power (now Petroleum), sole power to grant Oil Exploration, Oil Prospecting and Oil Mining Leases to Nigerian citizens or to companies incorporated in Nigeria. To further extend its hold on oil, an Offshore Revenue decree No. 9 provided that the Federal Military Government (FMG) should receive all offshore oil revenue from wells located in the coastal waters adjoining the oil minority states. An act that cut the oil minorities of the Niger delta off from any direct access to oil (Soremekun and Obi, 1993b:219–220).

Apart from divesting the oil minorities of the control of oil, the Nigerian state acting through the Land Use Decree of March 1978 (which later became the Land Use Act), later placed all land in the trust of the state government, again divesting the oil minorities of control over their land. What this meant was that the power over land resided in the state governor (under the military, an appointee of the federal government), who had the power to approve the issuance of, or revoke a certificate of occupancy in the "public interest". In 1993, the Babangida Administration further tightened federal control of land, when it promulgated decree 52 (Titles, Vesting etc.) which appropriated all lands within 100 metres of the 1967 shoreline of Nigeria. Like the earlier one, this decree also had a negative impact across the country and the Niger delta in particular. According to a recent Constitutional Rights Project (CRP) Report (1999) on the implications of the Land Use Act:

> Nowhere else in Nigeria has the impact of the Land Use Act manifested in all its imperfections and inequities, as in the Niger Delta region, Nigeria's main oil-producing region.

A similar position has been expressed by Oronto Douglas, an Ijaw Youth Council Activist, Lawyer and Deputy Director of Environmental Rights Action (ERA), when he is quoted (Don-Pedro, 1999b), as saying, that:

> No single piece of legislation in the country has robbed, in a more vicious manner, the people of the oil bearing Niger-Delta communities of their humanity than the Land Use Act of 1978.

Thus, not only was access blocked at the level of revenue allocation, but at the level of the ownership of (oil-rich) land. The Land Use Act as noted earlier took away from the people of the delta, their ownership, and occupancy rights in a land they had settled in, and lived on for generations, and long before the discovery of oil in 1956. In a region where land was of great significance as the basis of life, and a sacred trust being held by the living for future generations, the revocation of occupancy rights was seen as another unkind cut by the federal state against the oil minorities. Even the manner of the expropriation of their land left a lot to be desired. The people were neither consulted, nor was their approval sought, worse still, the main beneficiaries of the decree turned out to be the oil multinationals. It also foreclosed the demands the people could make on oil companies who acquired their land for "developmental purposes".

Having legally lost the ownership of their land to the government, the most the oil communities could claim from the oil multinationals was compensation or "surface rents" (covering assets on the surface—economic crops, fish, trees, etc.). The oil communities were not entitled to any royalties and taxes, and in the absence of fixed rates, the communities became bogged down in the politics of compensation. Indeed they had no control over the operations of the oil companies in their communities. The oil communities lost out either through the cornering of surface rents by a few influential elite, the low rates of surface rents and compensation, high costs and long duration of litigation, and inter-communal clashes over compensation or surface rights.

Another major grievance that emerged from the Land Use Act was the growing land scarcity, and the alienation of the people from their land as the oil industry expanded its operations throughout the delta and its continental shelf. According to an incisive report by Ibiba Don-Pedro (1999b):

> The major oil firm operating in the region, Shell Petroleum Development Company, SPDC, presently operates oil-mining leases covering 31,103 sq kilometres, a little less than half the entire Niger Delta. Combined with the space taken up by the other companies including Chevron, Mobil, Elf, Agip, Texaco, BP and Statoil, and Philips, considerable demand for land is a consequence of the presence of these oil-producing firms.

In a region interspersed with swamps, creeks, rivers and lakes, and where land is scarce relative to population size, the acquisition of land by oil multinationals deepened the scarcity; and reduced the quality of land. Activities of the oil industry such as seismic shooting, canalisation, gas flaring, discharge of waste waters, and oil spills contributed to the degradation of the fragile delta environment, with direct adverse impact on biodiversity, and the livelihoods of the people (Dappa-Biriye et al., 1992; Moffat and Linden, 1995; Omoweh, 1994, 1996; Ashton-Jones et al., 1999; Obi, 1997b). This was to contribute from the late 1980s onwards to communal strife over "scarce" land, community agitation against oil companies, and a climate of tension, violent conflict and anxiety in the delta.

Another critical issue emerging from the state take-over of land, was that most avenues through which the oil minorities could seek redress were constricted, frustrating, or even closed to them from the end of the civil war onwards. A case in point were the courts where the costs of litigation were very high and the poor villagers could neither match the wealth nor the staying power of the oil firms (Adewale, 1989, 1990). An often-cited example is "the Ekeremor-Zion, Ofoegbene, Obotobo and Sokebelou in which the communities sought to get compensation for a spill on their land which Shell blamed on sabotage. Succour came to the communities when the Federal Court of Appeal sitting in Asaba decided in their favour and awarded compensation amounting to N30 million. Their celebrations were however short-lived as Shell indicated its determination to plead against the judgement" (Don-Pedro, 1999b). In a bid to cut their losses, and as a result of their frustration with formal state and legal avenues, the people of the delta have sought to explore other means to seek redress.

At the end of it all, the oil minorities lost out in the struggles to control oil in post-civil war Nigeria. Even though more members of the elite gained access through the federal "benefactors" to the spoils of the oil economy, they did so mainly in their individual capacities, and the largesse never trickled down to the masses in their impoverished communities. This situation became worse with the immersion of Nigeria in a serious economic crisis, and the intensification of struggles over reduced oil rents. This also made the oil minorities abandon their passive resistance, by insisting on a fair share of the national (oil) cake. It is the bid by the oil minorities to recover this lost ground that largely propels the on-going conflicts involving the oil communities, the oil companies and the Nigerian state over the control of the oil-rich lands and waters of the Niger delta.

By controlling oil the federalist bourgeoisie which was a coalition of the victorious allies of the Nigerian civil war, excluded the oil minorities from oil, even if the bulk of this oil came from their region—the Niger delta. It also introduced the paradoxical element of the dependency of oil minorities on the hegemonic bloc in the federal government for access to the oil produced in the delta. Admittedly, more members of the oil minorities elite participated in the primitive accumulation of capital at state and federal levels, and played a gatekeeper role in the extraction of oil by oil multinationals, (as their faction of the Nigerian ruling class grew in size), but, this did not appreciably reduce their subordination to the hegemonic bloc of the federal elite. More fundamentally it did not lead to the emancipation of the toiling masses of the Niger delta in the oil-boom era. The centralisation of all oil revenues in the federal government reinforced the centripetal forces in Nigeria (Phillips, 1991:103), imposing thereby a military-unitary logic on an apparently federal system. The imposition of a centralist fiscal federalism on a mono-cultural economy meant that the other tiers of government were reduced to mere appendages of the federal government.

In the aftermath of the Nigerian civil war, contradictions deepened along the following lines: between the oil minorities and the (non-oil producing) majority ethnic groups, within the oil minorities themselves, between the "new" minorities and "new" majorities in the newly created minority states (Rivers and South-Eastern (later Cross River) states) leading to the agitation for more states. When eventually seven more states were created in 1976 none went to the minorities of the Niger delta. This worsened the contradictions between the oil minorities and majority ethnic groups, and between oil multinationals and the people of the oil producing communities of the Niger delta. These contradictions however did not explode, mainly because of the participation of a faction of the oil minorities in the sharing of oil surplus either in the form of government appointments, lucrative contracts, appointment to the boards of government parastatals and companies, or selection to represent the interest of the federal government on the board of oil companies. A lot depended on the balance of power in the social forces within the delta, between the delta and the national or federal level, and between the people of the delta and global oil capital.

Such benefits that flowed into the hands of the oil minorities elite fed into the reproduction of hegemonic class relations in the delta, which partly also gained from hegemonic relations at the federal level. The minority elite accumulated capital, becoming a bourgeoisie of sorts, dispensing favours and largesse in their local constituencies or in the cities, and providing legitimacy for the federal and national unity project in the Niger delta. Due to the benefits that accrued to them as allies in oil-based capital accumulation, they provided legitimacy for the activities of oil multinationals as agents of development. Even then the level of this support varied from one locality to the other depending on a host of factors and reflecting the depth of local contradictions.

As far back as 1970, the Ogoni Divisional Committee addressed a "Humble Petition of Complaint on Shell-BP Operations in the Niger Delta" to the Military Governor of the Rivers state, signed by some chiefs and members of the Ogoni elite. Its contents decried the loss of land to the oil industry, destruction of farmland—the Ogoni economic mainstay; destruction of the ecosystem, economic trees, fish and marine life, without any real compensation by Shell, lamenting that, "no attention has ever been paid to the fate of the poor people who bear the full weight of the national economic burden on their backs" (quoted in Saro-Wiwa, 1992). The Ogoni, one of the new minorities in the minorities' Rivers state exemplified the double-layered contradictions being spawned by the further integration of the Niger delta into the global capitalist system as a source of cheap oil, and that within the oil minorities on one hand, and between them and the federalist bourgeoisie on the other. The Ogoni elite who opposed their marginalisation soon fell back on the strategy of identity politics, mobilising the people to demand the creation of the Port Harcourt state.

Another critical point was the abandonment of the revenue allocation principle of derivation in favour of those of population and the equality of states after the civil war. The principle of derivation was based on the allocation of revenues on the basis of where it was derived from. From 1954 the principle of derivation was adopted (100 per cent) as an important basis for revenue allocation. From this point, the modality of sharing revenues between the various tiers of government (and regions) became highly politicised, and immersed in the struggles between factions of the ruling class. The reason for this is not difficult to fathom. Derivation was instrumental to giving the regional elite control of and access to the surplus generated in their region. Elite from poorer regions frowned at derivation in the name of the need to get an equal share of resources for balanced national development and a sense of belonging.

In the 1960s derivation was reduced to 50 per cent, alongside the setting up of the Distributive Pool Account (DPA). When the war broke out, under a national emergency the federal government took over the reins of fiscal federalism. As noted elsewhere, "through decrees 15 of 1967, 9 of 1971 and 6 of 1975, the balance of control and access to revenue tilted towards fiscal federalism at the federal level" (Obi, 1998b:265; Adebayo, 1988, 1993). Fiscal federalism accentuated the powerlessness of the oil minorities' elite, and their subordination to their partners at the federal level. The share of derivation since the end of the war shrank progressively from 50 per cent, down to 20, 1.5 and then was increased slightly to 3 per cent (administered by a federal agency—the Oil Mineral Producing Areas Development Commission) under the Babangida regime. The people of the Niger delta interpreted this development as a betrayal of the hopes they had nursed in supporting the federal side during the war.

Since most of the oil was contributed by the minority ethnic states of Mid-Western and South-Eastern Nigeria, the abandonment of derivation was interpreted as a treacherous ploy of denying those states the full benefit of their contribution to the federal purse. In reality, it was more of an intra-class struggle over which faction of the regionalist bourgeoisie (now broken up along state lines) would maximise the benefits from oil rents (Obi, 1998b:267).

In the 1979 elections which ushered in the Second Republic (1979–1983), both Rivers state and the South-Eastern state voted for the National Party of Nigeria (NPN) which was virtually a reincarnation of the old Northern Peoples Congress (NPC) and its southern allies. Yet, within each state the cracks widened, even if at the broad level, there was a measure of co-operation between the elite in the Niger delta and the dominant elite at the federal level. In Rivers state for instance, the elite from the other minorities complained of Ijaw (riverine) domination, while the elite from the "upland" groups began to agitate for a Port Harcourt state. In the same way, the Efik and the Ibibio elite struggled over power and resources partly by deploying politicised ethnicity, partly by exploiting linkages to federal power to provide leverage in their struggles. The Second Republic that was terminated by the December 31, 1983 coup did not lead to the creation of any new states. Neither did the Buhari-Idiagbon military administration attend to such demands before its own Chief of Army Staff, General Ibrahim Babangida, overthrew the regime in August 1985.

After the civil war, up till the early 1980s, most of the identity politics of the oil minorities was directed towards maximising access of the elite to oil surplus at the state and federal governments. The intra-elite struggles fed micro-minority movements operating mainly as social clubs, political caucuses, and pressure or lobby groups. There was no overt violence by an elite which accepted oil-based capitalist accumulation (and sought to participate in, and benefit from it) and a lot depended on persuasion. More fundamentally, the contradiction between global oil and local producers had not become glaring, even if the material condition of the people was worsening. It was not until the economic crisis of the 1980s that the trends began to change. At this time it was possible to discern a cleavage in the oil minorities movement. This was between those who benefited from, and supported the extractive state-global oil alliance, and those who were critical of the inequities embedded in that alliance. The masses were divided between these two tendencies and were to make up their minds only when the Structural Adjustment chickens came home to roost barely a decade later.

Economic Crisis, Structural Adjustment and the Changing Forms of Identity Politics of the Oil Minorities of the Niger Delta

The roots of the Nigerian economic crisis were embedded in the structural distortions sown during colonial rule, and the manner of the subordination of the Nigerian economy to the demands of the global capitalist market. This subordination consigned Nigeria to a peripheral position in the global economy as an exporter of primary goods and an importer of finished goods from the West. This external dependency rendered the economy vulnerable to crisis generated from the global markets. The immediate trigger for the Nigerian economic crisis was the oil-shocks of 1977 and 1981, in which the price of oil in global markets collapsed (Olukoshi, 1990:81–101). The oil-dependent, mono-cultural Nigeria economy was in trouble as a result of the refraction of the crisis in the global capitalist system locally. With foreign reserves barely enough to cover a few months of imports, the economy fell into dire straits. The shock absorption capacity of the economy had long been undermined by its weak import-dependent (light manufacturing dominated) base; years of mismanagement, waste and corruption, extraction by global capital and western commercial and oil interests, and two decades of military dictatorship.

The collapse of global oil markets alongside the devaluation of the dollar (in which Nigeria's crude is priced) meant a fall in oil exports and government revenues. According to Wright (1998:110), "during 1978 the country was earning $300,000 a day less in oil revenues compared with the previous year". When the first oil shock struck in 1977, the government of General Olusegun Obasanjo responded by announcing an austerity package amidst a balance of payments crisis. The austerity programme was based on reduced government expenditure and a low profile—a less ostentatious lifestyle for government officials. Operation Feed the Nation (OFN), launched by Obasanjo, called for a return to the land to grow food, rather than relying on food imports, providential oil windfalls (rather than on hard work), and white collar jobs in the boom cities. In 1978, the government raised two loans totalling about $2 billion from the Eurodollar market. This was partly encouraged by the need to address the imbalance in the external payments sector, the gradual recovery of the global oil markets, and pressures from external trade partners and economic advisers who felt that Nigeria was still under-borrowed. Thus, by the time Obasanjo handed over to the elected government of Shehu Shagari the economic crisis was well under way.

Yet, the full ramifications of the economic crisis were masked by the recovery of global oil markets, so much so that Obasanjo was able to hand over to Shagari an economy with external reserves worth about $3 billion and a debt service ratio of 1.5 percent. Shagari like his predecessor did not tackle the roots of the economic problems. Worse, his administration got carried away with the second (short) oil boom in 1980 and went on a spending binge. As a result, when the second oil shock struck in 1981, the economy virtually came to a standstill. The oil boom had finally gone bust, and the attempt of the Nigerian ruling class to use petro-dollars to import "development" had come to grief. The full impact of the global recession and an oil glut triggered Nigeria's economic and external debt crisis. According to Eghosa Osaghae (1995a: 24):

> With the glut in the world market, crude oil production fell steadily from 2.056 mbd in 1980 to 1.434 mbd in 1981 and 1.229 mbd in 1982. There was a corresponding decline in revenue collected by the federal government: from 15 billion Naira in 1980 to 12 billion Naira in 1981, and 11 billion Naira in 1982. The net value of exports declined from over 13 billion Naira in 1980 to 7.5 billion Naira in 1982; GDP fell by 5.9 per cent in 1981 (at 1977/78 prices) and by 3.4 in 1982; external debt rose from nearly 9 billion USD in 1980, to nearly 13 billion USD in 1982 and 18.5 billion USD in 1983; trade deficit was put at 2.1 billion Naira in 1982, with import bills of over 12 billion Naira, and by the middle of 1983, the total reserve was barely enough to pay for one month's imports at the prevailing rates; etc.

Shagari opened up discussions with the International Monetary Fund (IMF), and enacted the Economic Stabilisation Act of 1982, to arrest the speedy descent into crisis. By this time, the impact of the crisis in the external sector was fully refracted into the domestic economy. The revenues from oil exports continued to record a decline. According to Table 2, revenue from oil fell from 12,353 million Naira to 7,814 million Naira in 1982. By the time the government was overthrown at the end of 1983, it had fallen further to 7,253 million Naira.

Table 2. *Oil Statistics 1980–1993*

Year	Annual Output (millions of barrels)	Oil Exports (as % of Total Exports)	Revenue (in millions of Naira)
1980	753	96	12,353
1981	525	97	8,563
1983	470	99	7,814
1983	451	96	7,253
1984	508	97	8,268
1985	544	97	10,915
1986	534	94	8,107
1987	464	93	19,027
1988	507	91	20,934
1989	614	95	41,334
1990	648	97	55,216
1991	677	96	60,316
1992	619	98	115,392
1993	689	98	106,155

Source: Stephen Wright, *Nigeria: Struggle for Stability and Status*. Boulder: Westview Press, 1998, p. 108.

Shortage in government revenues meant that the various tiers could not meet their obligations. Contractors were not paid, workers were owed salaries for months, basic infrastructure could not be maintained, nor efficient services rendered. State schools were shut down as teachers went on strike after months of unpaid salaries, public hospitals had no money to maintain essential equipment and procure drugs, while the ruling elite intensified its struggles to get a greater share of shrinking oil revenues. Reduced welfare spending meant that the people had to pay more for education, health and basic services. Those who could not pay dropped out of school, took to self-medication or traditional medicine or lost their lives. When tariffs for basic services were raised, it was no guarantee of their reliability or their quality.

The picture in the private sector of the economy was equally dismal. The ISI strategy of development was crippled by the lack of access to foreign exchange with which to import raw materials, semi or fully processed goods and components, and badly needed spares. A lot of industries closed down for long periods, cut staff benefits in a bid to stay afloat, laid off or retrenched staff in their hundreds of thousands, and in some cases closed shop and left the country. The companies that survived operated far below their installed capacities and had large inventories of unsold goods as a result of weak demand in the domestic market. The automobile assembly plants, textile industries, consumer/light goods sectors which sourced a lot of their raw materials through imports were in crisis. A lot of indigenous medium and small scale industries collapsed, while oil multinationals and some of the multinationals involved in the import-export trade and consumer goods sector made profits. The impact of the economic crisis on the Nigerian society was devastating and provoked a lot of unemployment and suffering among the people.

Despite the economic reforms introduced through the Economic Stabilisation (Emergency Provisions) Act of 1982, the economy continued to plunge. Matters were not helped by the corruption that plagued the import license system viewed as a source of patronage and accumulation by the bureaucrats of the ruling party and their allies in the various arms of government, and its agencies. While the people suffered this insensitive group played politics with the economic crisis, either by denying outright that there was a crisis, blaming the opposition for exaggerating its magnitude, or adducing the crisis to an external source—the global oil glut—over which Nigeria had no control. The corruption of this elite and the intensified extraction of cheap Nigerian resources by global capital in collusion with local "gatekeepers", accelerated the decline into a full-blown crisis.

Shagari's negotiations with the IMF became deadlocked, due to the inability to reach an agreement on the following: the devaluation of the Naira, removal of oil subsidies and the privatisation of some critical state enterprises. As a result the government continued to struggle with the worsening balance of payments situation, blocked credit lines, increased opposition from various groups in society who were losing out as a result of the inability of the state to address the welfare needs of the people. On the domestic scene, the government resorted to repression to silence the opposition, relying on the upgraded and notorious Mobile Police Force to intimidate opponents and crush any public demonstrations, while the state-owned media spread government propaganda to all nooks and corners of Nigeria.

The hegemonic bloc of the Nigerian ruling class defended its capture of state office at all costs even as opposition was built up by the deepening contradictions in the crisis-hit oil economy. It resisted all efforts to be voted out of power in the 1983 elections when it manipulated the process, and intimidated the electorate to win so-called "landslide victories" across the country, including some critical opposition–controlled states. When it became clear that this bloc had lost all legitimacy to an opposition which was getting better organised, a faction of military generals struck on December 31, 1983, overthrowing Shagari's "democratically" elected government. General Muhammadu Buhari, a one-time oil minister, headed the new military regime.

Buhari and his deputy, Tunde Idiagbon had a "nationalist" response to the economic and external debt crisis. When talks with the IMF were also deadlocked, the regime resorted to oil counter-trade, an increase in the debt service ratio to 44 per cent, austerity measures, and the War Against Indiscipline (WAI) Programme targeted against all manner of social vices, waste and economic sabotage. The approach towards economic management was hinged upon a determination not to mortgage Nigeria to foreign interests, the rejection of some IMF economic conditionalities and the faithful implementation of government's austere economic reform packages. It was a rejection of the economic liberalisation or monetarist thrust of the International Monetary Fund and the World Bank, the donor community and the consensus within the dominant right wing circles in the western countries. Unfortunately, the measures adopted by the Buhari-Idiagbon regime failed to appreciably change the declining fortunes of the Nigerian economy. This in itself betrayed an improper appreciation of the nature of the Nigerian capitalist economy, while the regime's authoritarianism alienated the masses of the Nigerian people whose interests it was allegedly protecting. Thus, while resisting the forces of global finance capital, the Buhari-Idiagbon administration lacked an organised popular base, and did not address the root cause of the economic crisis. It was therefore hardly surprising that another faction of generals overthrew the regime in a palace coup in August of 1985. It was under the new head of state General Ibrahim Babangida that Nigeria started its march towards structural adjustment.

When General Babangida assumed power, the economy was virtually at a standstill, and external credit lines had been frozen by the creditor clubs in a bid to force Nigeria to the negotiating table with the IMF. The early measures of the government were basically populist in order to earn legitimacy and entrench itself in power. Some of these included the release of some individuals jailed without trial, repeal of some decrees which infringed on human rights, the release of politicians sentenced to long terms of imprisonment by the Buhari regime, and the encouragement of public debates on pressing national issues.

The journey towards adjustment took off with the appointment of an ex-World Bank employee, and economist, Kalu Idika Kalu, who was credited with having designed and successfully seen an adjustment programme through in Asia, as the Finance Minister. As a second step, Babangida threw open the question of reaching an agreement with the IMF and the World Bank to public debate. Across the country, popular groups mobilised themselves to oppose the Bretton Woods institutions on the grounds of their pernicious conditionalities, failure to cure the economic ills of any third world country, and the fact that agreement would amount to the re-colonisation of Nigeria. Academics, trade unionists, professionals, student unions, and social commentators were involved in the opposition to an IMF/World Bank programme for Nigeria. The private press carried editorials, feature articles, reports and scathing cartoons criticising the IMF, often portrayed as a doctor who gave the same medicine to all his patients, irrespective of the ailment, and eventually "nursing" them to death.

Babangida imposed a state of economic emergency on Nigeria in October 1985, through the National Economic Emergency Powers Decree (which gave Babangida full powers over economic policy), while the government worked covertly towards adjustment in national colours. The regime was under tremendous pressure from external sources to deregulate the economy. The fact that Nigeria's debt fell due in 1986, and needed World Bank approval for the rescheduling of these debts, placed the government in a tight position vis à vis mounting domestic opposition to an IMF loan. In the 1986 budget, Babangida implemented a critical IMF conditionality–the removal of subsidies in the prices of refined petroleum products by almost 80 per cent in one fell swoop. This was justified as a bitter, but necessary step towards economic recovery. The savings from the reduced oil subsidies would then be used to rehabilitate infrastructure, build rural feeder roads, boost agriculture and create employment for many Nigerians. This was followed a few months later by the implementation of yet another conditionality, the announcement of the plan to sell state shares in some parastatals.

On June 27, 1986 General Babangida announced the adoption of a "home-grown" Structural Adjustment Programme (SAP), which would last for two years. It was cleverly couched in terms of a temporary, but necessary self-sacrifice to salvage the nation, which should be supported by all Nigerians, especially as they had rejected an IMF loan. According to the 1996 Socio-Economic Report of the Federal Office of Statistics, SAP sought to pursue the following objectives:

- A restructuring and diversification of the productive base of the economy in order to reduce dependence on the oil sector and imports;
- An attainment of fiscal and BOP viability over the period;

- Laying the basis for a sustainable, non-inflationary or minimum inflationary growth;
- A reduction in the dominance of unproductive investments in the public sector (through privatisation and commercialisation) to improve the sector's efficiency and intensify the growth potential of the private sector;
- Achieving appropriate pricing by the removal of subsidies, especially those for petroleum products; and,
- Correcting the gross overvaluation of the Naira through the setting up of the foreign exchange market.

In July 1986, the Second Tier Foreign Exchange Market (SFEM) was established to set a market-determined exchange rate for the Naira (a euphemism for devaluation). This was followed by the deregulation of interest rates and later the scrapping of state agricultural marketing boards. More removals of oil subsidies followed (euphemistically called appropriate pricing), allegedly to curb cross-border smuggling of petroleum products, in reality a source of more surplus for state and oil capital. What was not obvious then was that this so-called home-grown SAP had the approval of the World Bank and the IMF, and included all the instruments and modalities of the standard IMF/World Bank adjustment programme. The reasons for Babangida's unsuccessful attempt to hide the external moorings of the SAP have been discussed elsewhere (Olukoshi, 1990). What is relevant in the context was that it marked a capitulation to the drive of global capital towards resolving the crisis of accumulation in Nigeria. This monetarist solution was imposed externally, but deliberately dressed up in home-grown colours in order to adopt a nationalist platform, which would knock the bottom out of the opposition of the popular classes, and confuse the people. In order to foreclose further debate the leading officials of the Babangida regime repeated the slogan over and over again, that there was no alternative to SAP.

The main plank of the opposition to SAP had been nationalist and popular. The reasons for this are not difficult to fathom. In the first place, the civil war and the oil boom had strengthened the nation-state project and the sense of national pride. The oil-boom had boosted the welfare role of the Nigerian post-colonial state, in which the masses of the people believed that they had a right to fully enjoy the benefits of oil. This feeling was enhanced by several wage increases, massive expansion in the educational, infrastructural, and bureaucratic sectors, and the hosting of cultural jamborees in the oil-boom years. It was therefore inconceivable for the people to accept a contraption imposed from outside that would wipe out the gains of the oil-boom years.

Secondly, they did not see any reason for paying the price of the corruption and profligacy of successive governments whose only legacy to Nigeria was the creation of a generation of millionaire generals, millionaire top bureaucrats in the public and private sectors, their cronies, contractors and pimps. Under SAP, the rich got richer and the poor got poorer. Worse, the industrial crisis, massive retrenchment, socio-economic hardships and debates had raised the consciousness of the people about how the shifting fortunes of the economy affected their lives. Increasingly, they began to recognise the need to defend the "social contract" between the rulers and the ruled, and prevent the re-colonisation of the Nigerian economy by those very forces that had historically underdeveloped Africa.

The Nigerian SAP was, therefore, in the mould of the orthodox IMF/World Bank Structural Adjustment Programmes. Even though it theoretically ended in 1993, when General Abacha replaced it with the so-called programme of "guided deregulation", the essence of orthodox adjustment has survived in Nigeria albeit in different forms. Among these are the expansion of the informal sector, the privatisation of the economy by the post-annulment ruling clique and their external allies, worsening economic crisis, and the virtually unregulated extraction of oil by western oil multinationals. Before going on to the impact of structural adjustment on Nigeria in general and minority identity politics in the Niger delta in particular, it would be apposite to examine some of the theoretical foundations of structural adjustment.

Structural Adjustment Programme in Nigeria: Theoretical Foundations

In order to understand the context and ramifications of the adoption of SAP as the sole panacea to Nigeria's crisis of accumulation, it would be important to examine the theoretical foundations of adjustment. In the first place, adjustment was a return to the classic notion of the free market (ruled by the invisible hand) via the monetarist route. Adebayo Olukoshi lucidly places adjustment in the "the context of the triumph of the monetarist shade of neo classical economics over Keynesianism" (Olukoshi and Nwoke, 1994:11). Keynesianism was hinged upon the role of the Interventionist State in fighting unemployment and regulating the market. It had emerged as a panacea during the Great Depression of the inter-war years.

However, after the Second World War, the prosperity of the 1950s and 1960s gave way to inflation and recession in the later half of the 1970s. A new thinking then emerged in neo-classical economics which laid emphasis on curbing inflation and a return to the rule of market forces (Olukoshi, 1990; Bangura and Gibbon, 1992). It identified inflation as the problem underlying the global capitalist recession, and saw salvation in the form of the shrinking of the state, reduction and regulation of money supply, deregulation of interest rates, trade liberalisation and giving free rein to the forces of demand and supply.

By the 1980s, a new thinking, monetarism, took the centre-stage of global economics. Olukoshi (1990) traces this to the rise to power in critical western European and North American countries of conservative, right wing governments (Margaret Thatcher in the UK, Ronald Reagan in the US, Helmut Kohl in West Germany, and Brian Mulroney in Canada). Side by side with this was the re-orientation of the IMF and the World Bank which abandoned their Keynesian outlook and embraced a monetarist agenda, the dominant influence of western countries in the IMF and the World Bank, and the crisis and collapse of the socialist mode of production in the Soviet Union and Eastern Europe.

The hegemonic ideology of monetarism thus became a driving force in the economic relations between the west and the third world, particularly Africa. Since the global recession of the 1970s sharply refracted into the African economies, the continent fell into economic and external debt crises. They were therefore subjected to a monetarist diagnosis and treatment. The African economic crisis was seen as the outcome of unbridled monetary expansion, excessive state intervention in the economy, imbalances in the external sector, and rent seeking among the statist and urban elite. Its panacea was therefore located in the "contraction of state activity and the development of liberalised markets" (Bangura and Gibbon, 1992:7). The IMF/World Bank rescue packages imposed on African states were therefore hinged on the logic of the market place and the retrenchment of the state. In order to achieve these the "conditionalities" imposed on African states pursuing economic reforms emphasised the devaluation of national currencies, economic deregulation and the reduction of administrative controls on the economy (Olukoshi and Nwoke, 1994).

The theoretical assumptions of global monetarism especially as they relate to the African crisis have not gone unchallenged. This challenge has come from neo-Keynesians, neo-Marxists, nationalists, scholars, popular forces, statesmen, and even international organisations such as the Economic Commission for Africa (ECA), which came up with an alternative framework to the Structural Adjustment Programme, called the AAF-SAP. A common ground for the criticisms of adjustment is its fetishisation of the market place or the invisible hand, its neglect of historical factors, and the role of external actors, thus rendering some of its conclusions a poor caricature of trends in the real world. Olukoshi and Nwoke (1994:22–23) aptly capture the Neo-Marxist critique:

> Quite clearly, the roots of the third world economic crisis are traceable to the host of structural distortions arising from their peripheral position in the world capitalist system.

The dangerous implication of the foregoing, the authors accurately note, is that adjustment "seeks to reinforce the very structures of dependence that were responsible for the crisis in the first place". The devaluation of national currencies and removal of subsidies raised costs and fuelled inflation, while the deregulation of interest rates, and foreign exchange rates fed into speculation and capital flight. Liberalisation contributed to the dumping of more competitive imports, the decline of local industries whose products were highly priced (relative to cheaper imports) as a result of high interest rates, inflation, and removal of subsidies. And so, since the imposition of adjustment in most African countries since the late 1970s, there has been a deepening of the economic crisis that SAP was meant to resolve in the first place. The same scenario has been replicated in Nigeria, where the adjustment became a part of the Nigerian economic crisis, with severe consequences for the growing crisis of governance.

External forces and their local partners drove the Structural Adjustment Programme of the Nigerian state. For the local bourgeoisie, what was at stake was its continued participation in globally led accumulation in Nigeria, on terms clearly laid down by its external partners. For the external partners, it was the quest to unfreeze Nigeria export sector, ease the export of capital and profit, while raising the "efficiency quotient" of capitalist accumulation through the further integration of the country into the global capitalist system. Thus, the economic reforms embarked upon by the Nigerian state were directed at a restructuring of Nigerian capitalism away from a command or state-centric economy to one in which the market prevailed. Policies on which

SAP was centred such as: devaluation, privatisation and commercialisation of state enterprises, deregulation of the economy and liberalisation of imports, removal of subsidies on petroleum products and fertiliser, and the manipulation of monetary instruments, were thus fashioned to open up the Nigerian economy to capital.

It has been strongly argued in some quarters, that SAP failed on most counts in Nigeria. A critical issue is that its theoretical premises were faulty and these contributed to a wrongheaded approach to economic reform in Nigeria. This much can be confirmed by the clear evidence that economic adjustment failed to come to grips with the reality of, and resolution of the Nigerian crisis. From 1986 when SAP came to life in Nigeria, the external debt profile has continued to grow, the quality of life of Nigerians has dropped drastically, while the economic crisis has in fact worsened. In a dramatic manner its harsh social consequences have fuelled misery, insecurity, tension and conflict within the country. At the level of governance, adjustment provided justification for one of the worst forms of authoritarianism in the history of Nigeria, even if this dialectically fed into the expansion of democratic space.

While there are those who lay the blame for the problem at the doorstep of poor implementation, and corruption of the Nigerian government, more perceptive observers have tied the failure of adjustment to its theoretical shortcomings, its anti-people policies and the virtual destruction of the welfare gains of the post-colonial era. The trickery and secrecy surrounding the adoption of adjustment, its pernicious conditionalities which resulted in widespread opposition by the poor and middle class amid state repression, underscore the hypocrisy inherent in the position that the problem was one of poor implementation, or those who claim that the consequences were "unintended".

The Impact of Structural Adjustment on Nigeria

As noted earlier, Structural Adjustment complicated the Nigerian crisis it set out to resolve in the first place. The introduction of SFEM in 1986 signalled the devaluation of the Naira. By December 1986, the Naira had depreciated by about 70 per cent putting a great strain on the Nigerian economy. According to a report by an agency of the Federal Government of Nigeria (Federal Office of Statistics, 1996:38):

> An examination of the economy during the pre- and post-SAP periods indicates that as at 1993, the quality of life in Nigeria was worse during the post-SAP era.

According to Toby (1992:27–32), after five years of adjustment, Nigeria was still in the economic doldrums. He supported his position by pointing to the low level of industrialisation, decline in capacity utilisation, high rate of unemployment, and the depreciation of the Naira by 1,750 per cent against the dollar, and over 4,500 per cent against the Pound Sterling. The massive devaluation of the Naira fed into an inflationary spiral. It raised the cost of production of local manufacturers, placing their finished products beyond the reach of most Nigerians, and making them less competitive than imported products. The high interest rates alongside the high cost of obtaining foreign exchange meant that manufacturers found it difficult to source imported raw materials. Although it could be argued that this forced them to look inwards, they were plagued by a host of problems including inadequate supplies, technological adaptability, high energy and infrastructural costs and depressed local demand which combined to lower capacity utilisation. The dream of the diversification of the mono-cultural basis of the economy remained an illusion, there was no appreciable increase in the proportion of non-oil exports, rather oil reinforced its dominance in the export sector (see Table 2). The cash crop boom expected to boost rural incomes fizzled out quickly, in the face of the escalating costs of agricultural inputs (particularly fertilisers), and the high costs of basic services, petroluem products and transportation. The situation was further worsened by the invasion of the countryside by middlemen who bought up produce for urban of even cross-border markets. Even speculators were not left out, as they found cash crops (particularly cocoa) an easy means of exporting capital from Nigeria.

Others (Phillips and Ndekwu, 1987; Ekpo, 1992; Adejumobi, 1995) have explored the various dimensions of the shortcomings of SAP. There is a broad agreement that its negative impact far outweighs the positive. Particularly painful, were the negative impacts of adjustment on social life. But before going into this, it is important to examine the impact on the debt crisis. The debt has continued to grow, while its external component has proved to be unmanageable. According to Table 3, before adjustment, in 1984, the total

Nigerian debt was 8,934 million Naira. By 1988, it had grown to 31,246 million Naira. Figures for 1998, ten years later, give an estimate of about $35 billion (3,150 billion Naira). With such a huge debt overhang, without a viable economic base outside the enclave foreign-controlled oil sector, the prospects for economic recovery appear bleak.

Table 3. *Nigeria's Debt (millions of Naira)*

Year	Total Debt Service	Total Debt Ratio	Total Debt
1980	774	4.2	8,934
1984	3,474	33.8	18,537
1988	2,178	33.4	31,246
1992	3,737	30.6	30,999

Source: Stephen Wright, *Nigeria: Struggle for Stability and Status*. Boulder: Westview Press, 1998:113.

The social impact of economic adjustment has been particularly harsh on the majority of Nigerians. First of all the collapse of the industrial sector, inflation and unemployment exacted a huge toll on the populace. The impoverishment of the middle class, the working class and the rural dwellers, led to a marked decline in the quality of life. Growing poverty also found expression in the widening gap between the rich and the poor (and the disappearance of the middle class). People began to gravitate towards multiple livelihoods, informal sector activities, religious and ethnic fundamentalism to survive, and give meaning to their materially weak existence. For the few rich, it was time to show off their wealth through lavish celebrations captured on prime-time television, land grabbing, putting up of magnificent mansions, the exhibition of automotive opulence, and a wild display of power. This aroused envy, hatred, withdrawal or desperation on the part of those without, contributing to the worsening of tensions in society. The rate of violent crime in the cities soared amid worsening tension and insecurity. In some of the campuses, religious fundamentalism and violent secret cult activities gained ground. Among the poor, diseases which were assumed to have been eradicated or brought under control, such as tuberculosis, returned in the face of declining living conditions, and the deterioration of fund-starved, ill-equipped and poorly-staffed hospitals.

During this period, many professionals in the specialised fields of medicine, engineering, and the social and natural sciences migrated to Europe, North America, Saudi Arabia, and South Africa, in search of better conditions of work and remuneration. Similarly, others with special skills—artistic and sporting—migrated abroad in search of greener pastures.

One of the most explosive reactions to SAP was the opposition to the "appropriate pricing" of petroleum products, one of the cardinal tenets of adjustment. The price of petroleum products has jumped in leaps and bounds by over 1,000 per cent between 1986 and 1993. The rationale given for "the removal of oil subsidies" is that the price of petroleum products in Nigeria is one of the cheapest in the world making the government lose a lot of revenue by selling cheap at home, when it can make a lot more via exports. The same position is behind the thinking that this cheapness of Nigeria's petroleum products is an incentive for the illegal export of these products to neighbouring countries which then exploit the wide price differentials to "subsidise" their economies. Apart from the need to cut losses from the sale of refined products, it was also justified as a source of increased revenue for the provision of infrastructure and welfare for Nigerians.

While it is clear that the Nigerian state is not subsidising petroleum products, what it erroneously refers to as subsidy is the opportunity cost of not exporting all the oil produced in Nigeria. As such the so-called appropriate pricing is no more than a consumption tax imposed on petroleum products. Apart from the widespread opposition to the increase in petroleum prices, which resulted in protests, demonstrations by students, workers and ordinary Nigerians, appropriate pricing has added to the socio-economic crisis. The increase was passed on to the final consumer in the form of increased transport costs, increased prices of food and manufactured products, increased tariffs for basic services, and increased charges for all services. The burden of appropriate pricing of petroleum has been heavy on the average Nigerian while those who are in charge of the state have billions of Naira at their disposal. A lot of the money has gone into the amassing of fortunes by a tiny faction of society, while the standard of living of the majority has deteriorated. It however dialectically fed into opposition to SAP, and the tiny minority that cornered the oil wealth. Such protests have been co-ordinated by organised democratic forces within civil society. The push and pull between these democratic forces and the authoritarian Nigerian state, particularly the hegemonic military faction have defined the broad parameters of democratic struggles in Nigeria from structural adjustment to date.

From the foregoing, it is also obvious that adjustment accelerated the worsening of the crises of governance and legitimacy that the Nigerian state was immersed in. Increasingly, the class character of the state was laid bare as a defender of the few winners in adjustment against the interests of the vast number of losers who were in the overwhelming majority. Its repression of any opposition to adjustment in the face of the glaring evidence of deepening economic crisis further alienated the state from the people, which even fuelled more repression. The fact that SAP was implemented side by side with a tightly-controlled political transition programme during the Babangida years, meant that some space was created politically for organised social forces to oppose the pernicious policies of the state, and its attempt to subvert its own political transition programme. Thus, groups such as the Civil Liberties Organisation (CLO) Constitutional Rights Project (CRP), the National Association of Nigerian Students (NANS), and occupational and nationality groups formed the critical part of the pro-democracy forces in civil society. They confronted the state head-on, and criticised its anti-people policies, further stripping it of its legitimacy as the "protector of all".

In 1993, after the annulment of the June 12 presidential elections, the government was buffeted on all sides by pro-democracy protests and a nationwide general strike was forced to "step aside", in August of the same year. Even then, the government did not leave without foisting on the country an unelected (illegal) Interim National Government (ING), headed by the retired United Africa Company (UAC) chief executive, Earnest Sonekan. The ING throughout its short-lived existence (August–November 1993) was under sustained pressure from opposition movements. However, these movements, beset by their own internal contradictions could not prevent another faction of military generals led by General Sanni Abacha (ING Minister of Defence) from seizing power in yet another palace coup.

The policy of Privatisation and Commercialisation through which state retrenchment from the economy was to be pursued threw up its own difficulties. In the first place, while some non-profit making government enterprises were left intact, profitable ones were sold, often to powerful individuals in government, their foreign partners, their front-people, or their friends. The same pattern of ownership by serving and retired bureaucrats and military officers of state-divested shares in publicly quoted companies, replicated itself through the various sectors. In the critical oil sector, the retrenchment of the state, through the sale of its shares in the downstream section merely reinforced the partnership between local and foreign capital. In the upstream sections of the oil industry, the impact of adjustment was the further dependence of the Nigerian state on the oil multinationals. On balance the state did not move out of its distributive and security roles, while foreign oil capital tightened its grip over Nigeria's oil.

Another problem thrown up by privatisation was that a lot of workers were retrenched in the so-called staff rationalisation exercises. In some cases the basis for retrenchment was unclear, and staff rationalisation became an excuse for witch-hunting, vendetta, creating openings for lackeys or courtiers, and distributing largesse to friends. Worse still, the commercialised enterprises were better known for the higher charges they placed on their services rather than the promptness of delivery or efficiency with which they carried out their duties.

There were complaints, that the distribution of state-divested shares favoured people from the southern part of Nigeria, who were allegedly dominant in the commercial and economic sectors. This caused some tension within the ruling class and fed into the slowing down of the deregulation of state participation in the private sector.

On a general level, the state continued in spite of SAP, to play a central role in the economy. In commercialised state enterprises, the state continued to control the management, appointing members of management board, dissolving and changing the board, or even replacing it with sole administrators accountable only to the presidency.

What the foregoing shows is that privatisation and commercialisation reinforced the factional struggles for access to resources and power in Nigeria. It also fuelled tension, mistrust and conflict between the "winners" and the "losers" within the context of adjustment. As such it provided a fertile ground for the resurgence of ethnicity as a mobilising or organising principle in the struggle between those who stood to gain everything and those who stood to lose everything.

Clearly, contradictions spawned by the economic crisis, and the superstructure of adjustment and authoritarianism had influenced the re-emergence of opposition movements, the democratic content of their demands and their effectiveness. This no doubt enriched the democratic struggle in Nigeria against well-entrenched forces of authoritarianism and extraction. The conflation of external and domestic factors no doubt cast a complexion on the struggles, but the site of the struggle remained in Nigeria. Nigerians as citizens made claims on a state that had clearly privileged external extractive interests over the welfare of its own people. They interrogated the state, and more critically the nation-state project, over what amounted to a betrayal of the dream of independence as well as the hopes the nationalist movement invested in a post-independence social contract founded upon the welfare of the masses. The post-civil war oil-boom accentuated such dreams and hopes, and for these to come to grief on the altar of SAP added potency to the quest of popular forces for a democratic and equitable resolution of the Nigerian crisis.

The deepening crisis of state legitimacy linked to authoritarianism, the widening gap between the rich and the poor, and the failure of the state to sustain the welfare gains of the immediate post-colonial and oil-boom eras, did not merely arouse democratic passions, it also contributed to the resurgence of ethnic identity politics. The overlapping of ethnicity and class provided a complex dimension to the political and social context of structural adjustment in Nigeria. As class cleavages widened under adjustment, so did overlapping ethnic identities become more competitive and conflictive. Struggles over resources, access to power and local autonomy, along ethnic, communal, and ethno-religious lines increased both in spread and intensity across the country (Osaghae, 1995a; Egwu, 1998). Although these struggles were often violent, resulting in the loss of life and property as in the cases of the Muslim Hausa versus Christian Katab in Zango Kataf, the Jukun-Tiv communal clashes, and the Muslim versus Christian riots in some towns in Northern Nigeria, and since 1993, increased tensions in Yoruba-Hausa relations, yet, it was not in all instances that ethnic conflict amounted to a regressive process, or the result of a return to primordial expansionist ambitions. In some instances, ethnic identity politics has been transformed through a process of renewal into a quest for social justice and local autonomy in ways that can promote a democratic project.

What is relevant to this study is the demonstration, that rather than focus excessively on "the disruptive and disintegrative tendencies of ethnic identity politics" (Lijphart, 1977; Rabuska and Stepsle, 1972), it is more rewarding to engage the concrete reality that the resurgence of ethnic identity politics in certain contexts, can be instrumental to a reconstitution of the nation-state project in Nigeria along democratic and equitable lines. Such contexts would be determined by the content of the demands of the social movements, the position of the productive forces in the globally determined relations of production, and the relative strength of such forces vis à vis the dominant national "coalition" and its external allies.

Ethnic Identity Politics under Structural Adjustment

SAP and Ethnicity: The Linkages

The ethnicity-economics interface as mediated by the political (especially the Nigerian state) was linked to the competition and conflicts between groups for an increased share of shrinking oil resources. Ethnic identity became a more critical key to survival, staking claims, and designing moves calculated to maximise the gains of entry, access and capture of power in a period of growing scarcities. Structural adjustment did not merely deepen existing contradictions in Nigeria's political economy in ways that worsened scarcities, its impact widened inequalities and disparities between individuals, groups and even regions. As such, a lot of premium was placed by political and social actors on either ensuring that the material basis of their reproduction was assured, or that if threatened or "stolen" they would fight to protect or win it back. Ethnicity under SAP was linked to the material basis of group, or factional survival, and was co-opted by individuals, groups and regions seeking the retention, or re-distribution of power.

Another critical intersection of SAP and ethnicity lies in the mediatory role of the Nigerian state, at the level of inter-group relations, and in terms of the social relations corresponding to oil-based capitalist accumulation in the country. From a historical perspective, the adoption of federalism was designed to preserve unity in diversity in a multi-ethnic Nigeria. This theoretically would give the constituent units a measure of autonomy, pooling their resources and energies to build a virile and united nation-state. The role of the state was therefore to act as a neutral mediator of the competing demands of the various groups and federal tiers. It was to integrate them as equal units into the march towards development and united nationhood. There was also the assumption that by creating various levels of autonomous space for representation, accumulation, and power (states and local governments), less destabilising forays would be made into central power, posing less threat to the stability of the federal state.

The foregoing expectations were totally misplaced in the Nigerian case. Being an offshoot of the colonial heritage with its bundle of contradictions and inequalities, the state was not a neutral arbiter between equal groups, and was immersed in class struggle and the accumulation of capital. It exhibited the hegemonic hold which a rather fluid and complex coalition of ethnic group factions (headed by the victorious post-civil war military) had over it. The very history of Nigerian federalism itself, the reality of militarism, and oil-based fiscal centralisation reinforced fierce inter- and at times, intra-group relations. Under adjustment, the state remained partisan, favouring individuals, and particular ethnic elite factions located in certain regions in terms of the distribution of power, resources and largesse. In the face of shrinking oil revenues, not only did mediation become more biased and repressive, it led to the marginalisation of the weaker members of the hegemonic ethnic coalition, and the exclusion and intensified exploitation of the weakest ones. The response of the marginalised and excluded, has been to mount pressure for redress, either by agitating for a restructuring of federal power, or seeking to assert more power over resources. At the same time excluded groups are defining their own political and social space in order to be better placed to stake their claims and resist the extractive forays of the Nigerian state.

Ethnic identity thus becomes a vital instrument, both for identifying the victims of marginalisation and exclusion, and for making claims on (and resisting) the Nigerian state. The case of the oil minorities who produce the oil, the country's mainstay, but are excluded from it underscores their protests and agitation for self-determination, which have recently assumed alarming proportions. The same politics of exclusion can be found in the interpretation given to the protests that trailed the annulment of the 1993 presidential elections won by Moshood Abiola a Yoruba, from the South west, by General Babangida, a Nupe from the North.

The role of the Nigerian state in oil-based accumulation has been discussed elsewhere (Ihonvbere and Shaw, 1998; Graf, 1988, Obi and Soremekun, 1995; Obi, 1997a, 1998b, 1999). What is relevant in this context, are the exclusion of the state from actual production, and its nature as a site of conflicting social forces. While the first enables us to grasp the role of the state as a "gatekeeper" in global oil-based accumulation, the latter, saves us from running the risk of treating the Nigerian state as an undifferentiated force. It is a site of struggles between various factions of the Nigerian ruling class, and between the state and the people, even while attempting to mediate these struggles. Its mediation of such struggles is not unilinear, but rather reflects the divisions within the ruling class and the balance of forces in society. The Nigerian state's gatekeeper role to foreign capital and its privatisation by a hegemonic bloc in the domestic fraction of the ruling class, broadly define its zero-sum politics, and the way(s) it responds to opposition and revolutionary pressures from below. It defends the interests of global and local capital, in ways that reflect the balance of power in society. In this way the capacity to mobilise forces using ethnic identity, as well as the class character of such forces become very relevant in the contest for power. Both factors made very important contributions to the changing forms of identity politics under economic adjustment.

The deepening of contradictions under SAP, as noted earlier contributed to worsening poverty, unemployment, land hunger and protests by excluded groups. These, as Osaghae (1995a), Adekanye (1995), and Egwu (1998) rightly argue, fed into the intensification of ethnicity and ethnic struggles over shrinking resources, power and the means of material reproduction. These factors themselves raised fresh problems for the state, especially in the areas of legitimacy and governance. The nature of these conflicts, and how ethnicity operated at the individual, group and spatial levels in Nigeria have been well explored, and need no further elaboration. What is important here is to analyse how the state mediated such conflicts.

Rather than respond directly to the contradictions and demands of these groups, the state relied on repression to crush all opposition to its policies and protect global oil. At other levels it adopted divide and rule tactics by deliberately provoking ethnicity, and ethnic conflict, especially where such conflicts would divert attention from the state, or its harsh policies. With the doors through which grievances could be addressed and redress sought shut, state repression, rather than cow all the people, dialectically fed into opposition groups engaging the state in democratic struggles. These complex struggles were waged at various levels, but often targeted the authoritarian state.

Having established the linkages between SAP and ethnicity, it will be necessary to take the analysis one step further, that is through looking at the aspect of ethnic identity politics. As noted earlier, adjustment sharpened the use of ethnic identity among competing elite. But it did not stop at that. Ethnic identity movements though complex, began to throw up a changing class character and balance of social forces. The "silent majority" no longer took the leadership of the ethnic elite for granted. Leadership was interrogated and judged by its ability to deliver to the masses, and where it was adjudged to have failed faced a stiff challenge by an alternate popular leadership. In other words, ethnic identity movements were not static, homogenous or class-neutral, as they contained contradictory tendencies, dynamics and factions.

What adjustment provided was a historical moment through which identity movements responding to stimuli in society would undergo transformation. The period of crisis, and the opportunities opened up by internal and external political developments; combined to expand the political space to include hitherto excluded social actors. As such, during adjustment, some identity movements were going through the motions of decay and renewal, responding to the challenges of individual, group, and class reproduction and the broader struggles for social justice, equity and power. There is no doubt that these struggles impinged on both the democratic and national question in Nigeria, and were to interrogate the inequitable (and militarist) homogenising process of nation building in the country.

Closely linked to the point made in the preceding paragraph, is the observation that in some parts of Nigeria, the SAP-ethnicity interface gave rise to ethnic identity movements of a decidedly popular character, whose demands were decisively democratic in content. One of such contexts currently throwing up such a popular character, is the oil minorities' question of the Niger delta in Nigeria.

The Changing Forms of Ethnic Identity Politics under Economic Adjustment: The Case of the Oil Minorities Movements of the Niger Delta

From the preceding section, it could be seen that ethnic identity politics in Nigeria under crisis and adjustment was soaked in rising ethnicity, tension, violence and conflict. This trend though found in all parts of Nigeria, was most concentrated and sustained in the volatile and oil-rich Niger delta. The raging crisis in the Niger delta that continues to spread and grow in intensity, has been the subject of national, and global attention since the early 1990s. At the heart of the conflict is the claim of the oil minorities to the right to control oil versus the counter-claim of the state and oil multinationals to exclusively extract and control the oil found in the minority areas of the Niger delta. The tensions and conflicts arising from claims and counter-claims to oil exploded in the face of the contradictions reinforced by SAP and authoritarianism. The frequency and intensity of conflict in the delta and the prominent profile of the state/oil multinationals versus the people dimension of the struggle captures the changing forms of ethnic identity politics in ways that become clearer in the rest of this analysis.

The Changing Global and Domestic Environment

The changing form of ethnic identity politics in the Nigeria delta has been largely shaped by the rapid transformations at the global and domestic environment levels.

At the global level, the end of the East-West cold war led to several changes. First was the virtual disappearance of the ideological battle, in the face of the retreat of communism, leaving the field open to the dominance of the neo-liberal capitalist ideology. This was articulated in a drive for a global neo-liberal revolution hinged on multi-partyism, the respect for civil and human rights, and the globalisation of market-based reforms hinged on "the spread and deepening world-wide of market forces and relations on a scale never before witnessed" (Laakso and Olukoshi, 1996:7).

The collapse of state socialism in Eastern Europe and the disintegration of large federations such as the USSR, followed by Yugoslavia, and the reunification of Germany, threw up hither-to suppressed currents of nationalism, ethnicity, religion and market relations, as these nations radically (and in some cases, violently) restructured themselves and attempted to climb out of the abyss of the crisis of socialist accumulation and the cynical misrule of Stalinist-type party bureaucracies. The resurgence of nationalism on a global scale while posing some problems for security and development did have a positive side in the legitimisation of minority rights and the right to self-determination. It was under this banner that the successor republics to the USSR won their independence, the Czech and Slovakia republics voted to go their separate ways, while the constituent republics of the federation of Yugoslavia are still rallying around this totem to ward off Serbian hegemony.

Another aspect, often overlooked, was the paradigmatic revolution in security thinking. Beyond the focus on military security of states, and cold war strategic calculations, the notion of security was expanded to include human, environmental and other non-military concerns (Obi, 1997b). An important aspect of this new trend was the attention paid to environmental threats to global security, and the ways through which these threats could be mitigated. Scholarly studies on this expanded notion of non-military threats to security blossomed in the West, particularly in the United States and Canada, and were, however minimally, to influence the inclusion of a humanitarian stake in foreign policy calculations after the cold war. Side by side with the concern for non-military threats to security, went an increased interest and indeed emphasis by international human rights and environmental rights and protection groups located in the West, on the promotion of a rights agenda in the third world. They provided a wide range of support, adopted causes based on the violation of rights in certain countries in the third world, and mobilised global opinion against the offending regimes and corporate actors, while empowering the oppressed people to uphold their rights.

The globalisation of information, the collapse and de-legitimisation of one man, one party or military regimes (with the remarkable exception of the Arab Gulf kingdoms and China) further accentuated the rapid political changes in the aftermath of the cold war, across the world. Another significant development was the emergence of regional blocs in Europe (European Union), North America (North America Free Trade Area), Latin America (Latin America Free Trade Area), South East Asia (Association of South East Asian Nations), as formidable players in an integrated global market place.

The ferment of transformations: political, economic and social in the wake of the end of super power rivalry provided a global canvas on which the forces for national and local transformations would play themselves out. These changes in themselves impacted on African states, which were immersed in the various stages of the crisis of legitimacy and governance.

The de-legitimisation of one party rule and military regimes, and the inability to exploit superpower rivalry to prop up dictatorships meant that a lot of African states, in the face of crippling economic crisis were forced to open up the political space to suppressed groups and forces. This opening up threw up a mix of forces, which in some cases won power in multiparty elections, while in others the incumbent "won" elections either by manipulating the state and electoral machinery, or by dividing and subverting the opposition. The main point however is that these transitions provided some space for hither-to suppressed demands, pent up rage and grievances, and demands for political restructuring to be expressed politically, and for groups as bearers of these demands to seek participation in the political process.

It was within this changing global context (with varied national reverberations) that the hither-to suppressed grievances of the oil minorities of the Niger delta burst forth. It was inevitable, that they would connect with the changing current of global transformations. Ken Saro-Wiwa (1992:7), the Movement for the Survival of Ogoni People (MOSOP) leader, and a martyr of the Ogoni resistance averred that:

> Three recent events have encouraged me to now place the issue before the world: the end of the Cold War, the increasing attention being paid to the global environment, and the insistence of the European Community that minority rights be respected, albeit in the successor states to the Soviet Union and in Yugoslavia. What remains to be seen is whether the same standards which they have applied in Eastern Europe will be extended to Africa.

The globalisation of local struggles in the Niger delta is a novel dimension of the ethnic identity politics in the Niger delta, and Africa. Unlike the old movement, the new was militant, and challenged the legitimacy of the Nigerian state, demanding its restructuring in a manner that recognised the rights of oil minorities to local autonomy and the control of their resources. Taking its case beyond the national to the global level for the first time required a host of new strategies, tactics, networking and politics. It was to some extent influenced by the struggles of indigenous peoples in other parts of the third world who were similarly struggling against oppressive states and big business. Yet the manner in which demands were mediated by the state and the local politics of global oil capital were greatly influenced by, and played out violently in, the domestic context.

The Background: Crisis, Authoritarianism and Resistance

The domestic environment within which minority identity politics assumed a more urgent profile, was one characterised by the crisis of Nigerian Federalism (Olukoshi and Agbu, 1996:74–101, Ihonvbere and Shaw, 1998; Amuwo et al., 1998). A lot has been written on Nigeria's political crisis aptly described by Oyediran and others in the authoritative volume entitled "Transition without End" (Diamond, Kirk-Greene and Oyediran, 1997). Therefore in this analysis, more emphasis will be placed on the domestic crises, political and economic, and those forces challenging the legitimacy of the Nigerian state, and seeking the restructuring of the federation.

At the core of the Nigerian crisis was the national question which underlined the growing disillusionment with the (centralising and homogenising) post-civil war Nigerian nation-state project, and the economic crisis with its harsh social ramifications. Increasingly, those groups excluded from access to power and resources by the monopolisation of power by a centralised federal state began to challenge its inequitable and exploitative basis. As Ade Ajayi (1992:14), a respected Nigerian historian put it:

> ... the National Question is the perennial debate as to how to order the relations between the different ethnic, linguistic, and cultural groupings so that they can have the same rights and privileges, access to power and an equitable share of national resources; debate as to whether or not we are on the right path to nationhood, debate as to whether our constitution facilitates or inhibits our march to nationhood, or whether the goal is mistaken and we should seek other political arrangements to facilitate our search for legitimacy and development.

The identity of a Nigerian citizen was no longer a mere given, it became a contested issue of gaining as a matter of right, equal access for all Nigerians to resources, and full participation in decision-making and the sharing of power. This provided a fertile ground for competing and conflicting identities. The very basis of the post-national unity project was rejected, as it tended to exclude people from certain parts of the country from enjoying certain benefits, occupying certain political offices and benefiting from the oil boom development projects of the 1970s and 1980s. A particularly touchy point was the way the "federal character principle" was applied. Lots of people though well qualified lost out in the race for admission to educational institutions, or gaining employment in the public service; while less qualified people from disadvantaged areas got an easy ride. Disenchantment further grew in the face of discriminatory policies against non-indigenes in the areas of admissions, jobs, award of contracts and even promotions in the civil service and armed forces. Indeed Nigeria's unity, bound as it is by (ropes of) oil, in such a climate of suspicion, alienation and anger has been very fragile and tenuous.

As such by the time the bitter effects of adjustment brought the economy to its knees, those who lost out in the distribution of privileges and were discriminated against despite being full blooded Nigerians lost faith in the national unity project as a farce intended to legitimise the monopoly of power by the elite from a particular section of the country. Groups emerged to articulate the need for a re-negotiation of the very basis of the Nigerian federation and place this issue on the front burner of national discourse. Thus, the Nigerian state caught in the global gale of political liberalisation in the 1990s was buffeted from all sides by "re-assertion of ethnic and religious identities whose single-minded suppression was central to the earlier efforts at promoting nation-building"(Olukoshi, 1996:7).

The Babangida political transition and the structural adjustment programme reinforced the tensions within the Nigerian nation-state, and the hardships borne by the majority of Nigerians through its authoritarian and deceptive tactics. More than ever before, religious and ethno-regional considerations re-asserted themselves with a vengeance as resources grew smaller, and marginalised groups sought redress. These struggles involved the various political units and nationalities making up the Nigerian federation.

Controversy also broke out when the country covertly joined the Organisation of Islamic Countries (OIC), in spite of its official policy of secularity, pitching Christian against Muslim organisations in a very emotional debate. Matters were not helped when the perennial religious riots broke out in the north, along with a rash of other communal clashes. At the same time the restive communities in the Niger delta had begun to seethe. At the heart of their demands, were protests against a federation structured against their interests, survival and development, compensation for the destruction and pollution of their lands and waters by oil multinationals, and their right to control their own resources. In extreme cases, such groups began to push for a radical restructuring of the federation to give more autonomy to ethnic groups, while drastically reducing the power and resources at the disposal of the central government. The harsh repression of these demands for political restructuring and anti-SAP protests by the ruling military have only added more fuel to these struggles which are not without legitimacy in the light of the (new) global emphasis on democracy and human rights, and the quest for meaning and survival in an increasingly globalised economy.

Some of the markers for the rising tension and conflict within Nigeria were as follows: the possibility of a break-up of the federation under pressures for local autonomy and control of oil resources, agitation for changes in fiscal federalism and a return to the allocative principle of derivation, mounting criticism of the federal character principle and the increased intensity and violence of ethnic, religious, and sometimes, communal conflict. In spite of the federal reforms under the Murtala-Obasanjo regimes, strong ethno-regional undercurrents continued to dominate elections especially at the state and federal levels. The race to elective office became an electoral war, or in real terms a political war in which ethnicity was freely deployed by factions of the elite. These calculations featured prominently in the 1983 and 1993 federal elections, and were not too far beneath the surface in the recently concluded 1999 federal elections. A rather frightening dimension reared its head on April 22, 1990 when Major Gideon Orkar, a middle-ranking officer of the Nigerian army in a broadcast announced not just the overthrow of the Babangida regime, but the excision of the seven Hausa-Fulani dominated states from Nigeria. Later events showed that Gideon Orkar had acted with other officers and friends from the ethnic minority areas of Northern and Southern Nigeria aggrieved by the domination of power by the "core" North. Even though the coup failed, it succeeded in bringing to the fore, the level of disenchantment over perceived ethnic (Hausa-Fulani) domination in the Nigerian federation.

The orthodox measures of diffusing power and resources to the other tiers: the creation of states and local governments, and mediatory agencies or development parastatals did not go far enough, and in many cases worsened old anxieties, and created new conflicts in the zero-sum contest for power and resources. This was mainly because in all the orthodox measures adopted by the federal government, there was no real devolution of power to the other tiers of government. The federal government kept a tight leash on the process, by controlling security, funding and the appointment of the chief executive and members of the executive board of mediatory agencies as a means of distributing largesse and rewarding its cronies.

Right from the era of the Niger Delta Development Authority in the 1960s, to that of the post-war Committee for the 1.5 per cent Ecological Fund of the 1980s nothing much was done to attend to the complaints of the oil minorities. When villagers from Iko in 1987 carried out a mass demonstration against Shell neglect in what can be described as one of the earliest attempts after the end of the Nigerian civil war, at a popular uprising in the delta, mobile policemen were invited in by Shell. The mobile policemen embarked on a punitive expedition in which several Iko villagers were shot dead, many arrested, and houses were looted and destroyed. Although investigations followed the brutal assault on Iko by the Nigerian police, nothing was done, either to compensate the affected villagers, repair the damage inflicted on the village, attend to their grievances or even bring the trigger-happy mobile police men to book (ERA, 1995).

It was not until June 1992, after armed anti-riot police invited by Shell to quell a peaceful demonstration by villagers carrying leaves had ended in the razing of Umuechem, a community not far from Port Harcourt; and the murder of scores of villagers by rampaging armed mobile policemen (Abimboye, 1990; Rowell, 1994), that a presidential delegation toured the delta to learn first-hand about the people's grievances. A judicial panel of enquiry was also set up by the Rivers state government to investigate the Umuechem incident and make recommendations (Inko-Tariah, et al., 1990; Obi, 1997a). The outcome of the tour by the presidential delegation was the announcement by the then Nigerian Vice President, Vice Admiral Augustus Aikhomu recognising "the need to increase the government's involvement in ameliorating the environmental and ecological degradation of these communities as a result of the exploration and exploitation of crude oil" (Gbadamosi, 1992:28). General Babangida soon after announced the establishment by decree 23, of the Oil Mineral Producing Areas Development Commission (OMPADEC), on July 10, 1992.

To assure full federal control, OMPADEC was placed under the presidency, its first director-general though an indigene of Rivers state, was a former director of the Nigerian State Security Service (SSS). In addition, all the members of the OMPADEC board were appointed by the presidency and were strictly not the elected representatives of the oil producing communities of the Niger delta. Similarly, the Commission was fully funded from the 3 per cent derivation fund controlled by the federal government. Indeed, some of the members of the board were from non-oil producing parts of the country. Like earlier official policies towards the Niger delta, OMPADEC was a gesture of tokenism. It ended up as a conduit pipe for the federalist bourgeoisie and its oil minority allies, and portrayed a grand strategy of destabilising the oil producing communities of the delta through divide and rule tactics. Worse, the limited contributions that OMPADEC could have made, were hampered by institutional instability and crisis. OMPADEC's first chief executive was removed from office after numerous petitions and allegations of corruption, and he fled abroad shortly after. His successor also from the delta—an indigene of delta state and a businessman and politician—spent the better part of his term handling the crisis he met, before he too lost out in the bitter politics of the presidency. A new OMPADEC chief executive has recently been appointed, and so far he is engaged in putting out many fires, including the payment of a huge backlog owed to contractors, who have formed a pressure group to articulate their objectives, and collect their money.

Through its distributive policies OMPADEC was able to play one community against the other, pitch one ethnic group against the other, and place clients of the state: elite and traditional; in positions of advantage in the award of contracts and placement in powerful positions. Communities engaged themselves in low intensity conflicts over the location of OMPADEC projects, while others were practically torn apart over the choice of a project, or between those who rejected the project, and those who wanted it. OMPADEC in the tension-soaked environment went on to identify, and collect information on the activities of "troublemakers". In most parts of the delta, OMPADEC had no serious impact, and was viewed with suspicion. A lot of the projects were abandoned, contractors were owed large sums of money, at a time when OMPADEC funds were allegedly diverted, while the siting of projects further worsened the tense intra-communal, inter-ethnic politics of the delta. It was perhaps hoped that these would divert attention from the federal state and the oil multinationals, but it achieved the exact opposite. Partly due to OPADEC's inability to deliver, even more pressure was mounted on the state by those oil minorities movements which clearly transcended the trap of inter-communal feuding to wage one of the most concerted and popular struggles against the state and global oil.

Perhaps the greatest weakness of OMPADEC was that the people of the oil producing communities were totally excluded from its decision-making processes. This was further compounded by the corruption and its lack of accountability to the people of the oil producing communities. The lack of transparency and divide and rule tactics of its operations soon marked out OMPADEC as part of the infrastructure of federal hegemony in the Niger delta. It to all extents and purposes became yet another local site in the Niger delta for primitive accumulation, and intra-elite struggles for office, power and contracts.

On balance, OMPADEC had no positive impact on the wretched state of the oil communities, except, in the words of Don-Pedro (1999a:15), "to produce millionaires of a few contractors and members of the traditional ruling class in the oil producing areas". The creation of a few millionaires and more office holders, did not positively affect the overall quality of life in the impoverished villages, it worsened matters, as the few rich elicited a mixture of envy, hatred, scorn and admiration. This combustible mix combined with existing rivalries, cleavages and perceptions of betrayal to explode into complex conflicts at the personal, intra-elite and national levels.

A lot of attention was focussed on the oil-rich federal state which monopolised the control of oil revenues and political power even as it continued to create unviable states and local governments which were absolutely dpendent on federal allocations, and lacked any real power. The impact of all the pressures on the federal state to decentralise its grip over oil and society and the frustrations of marginalised groups has compounded the national crisis. A direct consequence of this development, is the raising of the stakes in the contest for power at the centre, and the determination of the losers to either insist on the political restructuring of the country, or the right to secede. The inability of the ruling elite through a process of bargaining and agreement to arrive at a just and equitable modality for sharing oil revenues is a critical aspect of Nigeria's daunting national question.

Three developments were most critical in the worsening crisis of the Nigerian state: the class struggles around oil, the annulment of the June 12, 1993 presidential elections by General Ibrahim Babangida, and the hanging of nine oil minority-rights Ogoni activists, including Ken Saro-Wiwa, by the military junta of General Sanni Abacha. Most dangerous perhaps was Abacha, under whose regime, governance assumed a macabre dimension of personalised rule, in which the nation swayed precariously on a knife-edged precipice sharpened by the reality of a forced unity and the prospects of a forceful disintegration.

The class struggles around oil were more intense and violent as oil revenues shrank progressively in the 1990s and as the value of the Naira fell. These struggles pitched various factions of the elite against each other, those who had "captured" the federal state against the "outsiders", and those who had the legitimate monopoly of the means of organised war (state violence) against the civilian elite. At a more critical level, they pitched popular groups against the state, the statist elite and foreign capital. These contradictions and struggles became more acute when the state manipulated both programmes of political and economic liberalisation to reinforce its position in oil-based accumulation, while suppressing all opposition to the programmes.

A crucial development was the increasingly popular character of the struggles against the state. Popular organisations in civil society such as the labour force, students, professionals, market associations and human rights groups opposed policies such as the appropriate pricing of petroleum products, which they saw as an oppressive tax. Being forced to pay internationally competitive prices for petroleum products locally was seen by most Nigerians as a violation of their right to enjoy one of the gifts which nature had endowed the country with. It also went some way in undermining the legitimacy of the state, which by extracting more from its already impoverished people was clearly violating one of the principles on which the post-colonial social contract was based, and upon which post-civil war public welfare policies rested.

Apart from the mainstream popular groups involved in the opposition to the authoritarian state, some other groups began to show a strong pattern of transformation by the politics of structural adjustment. This reflected in the democratic content of their demands, and the popular social base of their support. Emerging trends in the politics of the minority ethnic groups of the Niger delta beginning from the late 1980s, and continuing to the 1990s underscored the transformations taking place within the social movements of the Niger delta as they mobilised to resist marginalisation, exploitation and other threats posed by the state-global oil alliance. A note of caution must be made to the effect that these transformations did not and do not suggest a total break from the past, or a complete transformation in social relations in the delta. What they do capture is the emergence of strong social forces from below, fully supported by the people, and charting an alternate course of liberation under a "new" alternate radical leadership. The new bearers of the struggle emerged along the lines of a radical ideology of oil-producing nationality liberation from "internal colonisation" (Naanen, 1995:49–50), a radicalised elite faction, the youth, women and the organised masses. They operated through new mass movements operating outside political parties, and the traditional structures of governance, local authority and control.

The move towards mass oil minorities movements has been met with resistance from certain quarters: the oil minorities elite factions aligned to the federalist bourgeoisie, the traditional elite aligned to the federal state and acting as local gatekeepers for the oil multinationals, and the militarised federal state ever so intent on the monopolisation of oil power, and the equivalent "Midas' touch" it bestows on those who capture state office. It is a zero-sum contest in which the monopolists and the popular forces of local resistance are locked in battle. Both sides have reached out to local and global allies who have joined the fray, turning the oil-rich Niger delta into one of the most contested terrains of global accumulation in the world.

Regarding the impact of Babangida's farcical transition or "transition without end" (Diamond, Kirk-Greene and Oyediran, 1997), on Nigerian politics, a lot has already been said on how the programme tried, through twists and turns, to subvert the democratic basis of the transition, an act that peaked in the annulment of the widely acclaimed June 12, 1993 presidential elections, midway through the announcement of the results. The grand design of the personalised rule project of Babangida, and the cynical Machiavellianism that underscored his mode of governance coupled with the vicious repression of any opposition to the project and other unpopular state policies suggested that a real transition under Babangida, could be nothing more than another political illusion.

The political process was closed to all those opposed to the personal rule project, and even when they managed to enter the two government registered, funded and administered parties, they were systematically frustrated by being banned, unbanned, harassed, and compromised, all in a bid to frustrate them out of the race, or buy them over. The political space and political institutions through which the people could make demands upon, and participate freely in the political process were either destroyed, in retreat, or were dominated by the personalised state. Thus, the way was left open, for political jobbers, opportunists, civilian sycophants and lackeys of the military, and those willing to subordinate themselves to the personal rule project of the incumbent military president. A lot of the outspoken politicians, critical journalists and pro-democracy activists found themselves in detention, in hiding or on the run from members of the security forces who were let loose to "secure" the country for the perpetuation of military rule. Yet, it was under this suffocating climate of authoritarianism that associative movements with a strong pro-democracy thrust flowered. Their strategy was to create and exploit autonomous space outside of the state to push a popular democratic project. It was they who mobilised the people to protest against harsh and unpopular policies, violation of human rights, and to resist the self-succession plan of General Babangida. Setting up contacts locally, and within the international community, they sensitised everyone to the fact that democracy was on trial in Nigeria, and everything had to be done to defend democracy.

This period also coincided with the resurgence of ethnic identity politics in the delta and popular uprisings against the state and the oil multinationals especially Shell. Leading the way was the Ogoni Bill of Rights (OBR) of 1990 (and the 1992 addendum to the OBR) making specific demands for local autonomy, compensation for pollution, and reparations for unpaid royalties to the people, on the Nigerian government and Shell. These demands went unacknowledged, and tensions continued to mount. In addition to the notorious case of the Umuechem massacre in 1990, Rowell (1994), documents the spread of protests in the Niger delta: Ogbia, 1992; Igbide, 1992; Uzere, 1992; Diebu, 1992; Burutu, 1992; Bomadi, 1992 and Irri, 1993. These are apart from the well known case of Ogoni protests (Boele, 1995; Amnesty International, 1993; Maier, 1993; Garner, 1994; Sorunke, 1994; Newswatch, 1993; Robinson, 1996:58–80), and the reported sacking of Obagi, Brass, Nembe Creek and Rumuobiokani, by the mobile police force invited by oil companies to "protect" company property from protesting villagers (Crow, 1995; Amnesty International, 1993; Ibeanu, 1997, 1999).

During January 1994, another federal ministerial team toured the Niger delta. It was led by Donald Etiebet Minister for Petroleum Resources, Michael Ibru, Minister for Internal Affairs and Melford Okilo, (ex-Rivers state governor) Minister for Commerce (all ethnic minorities of the delta). They collected memoranda from aggrieved groups, felt the pulse of the people, and appealed for calm; after which they presented a report to the authorities at Abuja. Like other delegations before them, the Etiebet group empathised with the plight of the oil producing minorities of the delta, but beyond this, nothing fundamental was done to change the unhappy lot of the people, and ease tensions building up in a region that supplied the precious lifeblood of the Nigerian state.

It is important to note that in relation to the grievances and demands of the associative movements that emerged in the Niger delta, Babangida's response was one of repression of the movements. His other major response was to resort to handling of oil minorities' demands in ways that emphasised federal power through programmes that failed to address the fundamental issues, and concentrated rather on the funnelling of funds to government clients in the delta. The Ogoni Bill of Rights (OBR), the addendum and demands made by other mass-movements in the delta were ignored by the federal government, which instead added insult to injury by repressing the movements. For instance, all regional and nationality-based political organisations were banned in a bid to de-legitimise and de-politicise the oil producing nationality movements in the Niger delta. Well before this, the government in 1987 had enacted the Civil Disturbances (Special Tribunal) Decree that sought to curb all forms of civil unrest, especially those directed against the state.

The fact that this bid to repress the oil minorities failed is clearly manifested in the activities of the Association of Mineral Oil States (AMOS), the Ethnic Minority Rights Association of Africa (EMIROAF), the Association of Oil Producing Communities of Nigeria, the Southern Minorities Movement (SMM) and the Movement for the Survival of Ogoni People (MOSOP) in the early 1990s. Though AMOS collapsed under an onslaught by the government and its local clients, MOSOP continued to wax stronger and its example soon spread to other oil producing communities in the delta. By May 1993, close to the handover date, the military government enacted another decree designed to destroy the basis of oil minority struggles in the Niger delta. According to the Treason and Treasonable Offences Decree of 1993, minority agitation for self-determination was pronounced a treasonable offence, punishable if found guilty, by death. It was followed in 1994, by the enactment by the Rivers state government of the Special Tribunal (Offences Relating to Civil Disturbances) Edict, under the Civil Disturbances (Special Tribunal) Decree of 1987, which ousted the jurisdiction of normal courts and granted the sole power of appeal to the Provisional Ruling Council (PRC) of the federal military government. It was under this decree, that Ken Saro-Wiwa and his co-activists were to be charged, found guilty and hanged in 1995. Following the decree and edict came the increased militarisation of the delta and the entrapment of activists, in order to enforce order and enhance extraction. It then meant that while the door to dialogue, access and power remained firmly shut, they had lost the right to organise and protest their marginalisation.

It was their attempt to resist extraction and repression under the Babangida years, and force through a project of local autonomy that transformed the oil minority ethnic groups into oil minorities' nationality movements. Their claim to "nationhood" was not so much an act of secession as it was an act of the rejection of an alienating, exploitative militaristic and monopolistic federal project. Counter-nationalism or micro-nationalism not only provided a refuge or platform for the solidarity of the oppressed and excluded, it gave a political identity and historical appeal to the social forces seeking liberation, by defining their goals in (ethnic) national terms. Politicised ethnicity became the armour of the oil minorities, offering protection, protesting discrimination, exploitation and injustice, and mobilising these complaints into a rallying force of all forces seeking the "de-colonisation" of their oil-rich (ethnic) nations.

Under MOSOP's leadership, and after the federal government and the oil multinationals did not respond to the demands of the OBR, and its addendum, the Ogoni people did not only proceed to protest, they used their blocking power to attract the attention of Shell, which continued to deny any responsibility for the plight of the Ogoni. In the face of Shell's denials of ecological irresponsibility and exploitation of the Ogoni, using all kinds of contorted arguments, and blaming the Ogoni for sabotage and seeking attention by exploiting Shell's visibility and vulnerability, the people became even more determined to take on Shell. By May 1993, despite the militarisation of the delta, and the activities of the local gatekeepers, popular forces forced Shell out of Ogoni, abandoning its equipment, but operating its pipelines automatically. Shell's symbolic retreat in 1994 from Ogoni (9 oil fields and 96 production wells) was a moral victory for the Ogoni, and demonstrated to them that they could take on one of the world's richest and most powerful multinationals, Shell, and win. For Shell, it was a humbling experience, and newspapers in Nigeria (Lukula, 1994; Izeze, 1994), carried stories of the huge daily losses (28,000 barrels/day, valued at N9.9 million daily) Shell was suffering due to the "stoppage" of its operations in Ogoni, and the loss of equipment in its five flow stations in Ogoniland: Yorla, Bomu, Korokoro, Bodo-west and Ebubu.

The people had effectively used their blocking power against Shell, providing them a basis for more, but very costly struggles. But it did show other oil producing communities, that Shell, the biggest, oldest and most visible oil multinational in the delta could be de-mystified. Six years later, MOSOP stills bars the gates to Shell's re-entry into Ogoni, and Shell, for its own part has let it be known that it will not operate behind a military shield.

When the presidential elections pronounced free and fair by local monitors and international observers were annulled, democratic forces in civil society fought the annulment, forced Babangida to leave power in August 1993, but lost the battle to reverse the annulment. What followed: the foisting onto the country of an illegal Interim National Government, the November 17, 1993 "silent" coup that ushered General Abacha into power, only served to deepen the Nigerian crisis, and increase the stakes and tensions in the Niger delta.

As recent revelations in the Nigerian and international media show, the Abacha regime was one of the most corrupt military governments in recent Nigerian history. Like the Babangida regime it gained great notoriety at home and internationally for the wanton violation of human rights. The agenda of the personalisation of power and personal rule assumed a greater and grotesque profile, matched only perhaps by the unprecedented ferocity with which state terror was visited upon any opposition, real or imagined. Politics was crudely reduced to a war in which the state firmly in the grip of the new maximum ruler was used firstly to amass (oil) wealth, and concentrate power in the person of the head of state to intimidate, compromise or buy out, repress or outrightly crush opponents of the regime. By the time Abacha rolled out a new transition after truncating Babangida's unfinished transition, it was clear to the discerning, that Nigeria had entered into a new phase of horror in imperial militarism, complete with its band of loyalists: praise singers, intellectual pimps, Rasputins, bouncers, jobbers, points-men and foreign interests, all keen on making a killing in the new emperor's fief (Nigeria).

It was a final onslaught against the remnants of the democratic forces in civil society that Babangida had tried so hard to destroy, without success, and which had picked up the gauntlet once it became clear that General Abacha had no interest in de-annulling the June 12 elections, nor in releasing the winner of the elections, Moshood Abiola arrested in 1994 for declaring himself President and insisting on the sanctity of a mandate given by the Nigerian people. The full might of the state descended on the pro-democracy movement in Nigeria. At the same time there was the sustained official campaign to regionalise and give the pro-June 12 movement an ethnic coloration. It was projected falsely as a narrow agenda of Southwest Nigerians (the Yoruba), who wanted to destabilise the country because of an election that "had been overtaken by events".

It was in this context of extreme tension and an onslaught against pro-democratic forces, that the state confronted the oil minorities movement of the Niger delta. To the federal government the activities of these groups was a big threat, especially as their growing blocking power was interrupting oil production (and accumulation) and attracting a lot of local, and worse still, international attention to the crisis brewing in the Niger delta. In particular, the activities of MOSOP were interpreted not just as being subversive to oil-based accumulation, but a most dangerous example to other oil producing communities in the delta; and other aggrieved ethnic nationalities in the federation. There was also a strong suspicion that the "revolutions in the delta" could end in a possible secession, and a cutting off of the fiscal basis of monopolistic control of federal power and a homogenising nation-state project. On a final and desperate note, the "MOSOP revolution" was interpreted as a direct challenge to the personalisation of the power project, as MOSOP leaders continued to stick to their guns after several arrests, detentions, meetings with state officials, and finally, direct warnings.

In order to crush the uprising in the delta, the region was occupied by the military, further raising tension in an already charged atmosphere. This force initially made up of mobile police men was later replaced (absorbing also, the mobile police into its operations) by regular soldiers from the Nigerian Army, and re-named the Rivers State Internal Security Task Force. This force was placed under the command of Major Paul Okutimo. Under Okutimo's command, protesting villagers were shot, beaten, arrested, their houses razed or bombed and properties looted by troops deployed to enforce order in the delta (Robinson, 1996:58–61; Boele, 1995; CLO, 1996). Okutimo it was alleged, citing an intercepted memo to the Rivers state military administrator, dated May 12, 1993, and titled, "Restoration of Law and Order in Ogoni", had recommended "wasting operations coupled with psychological displacement", as methods of dealing with the Ogoni.

In Ogoni, there were shootings in Biara village on April 30, 1993 when Nigerian security forces opened fire on villagers protesting the destruction of their crops and farms by Wilbros, an American oil service company laying pipes for Shell. Many villagers received gunshot wounds, while in another related incident a man Agbarator Otu was shot in the back and died during another incident at Nonwa, involving peaceful demonstrators and federal security forces. In between, Ken Saro-Wiwa was arrested and detained, and closely monitored by members of the security forces (and Shell). In spite of this, Saro-Wiwa, together with his supporters in MOSOP, particularly the National Youth Council of Ogoni People (NYCOP) successfully mobilised for an Ogoni boycott of the June 12, 1993 Presidential elections, to demonstrate their non-recognition of the legitimacy of a federal government (operating under an undemocratic 1989 constitution) that was oppressing and robbing the Ogoni of their oil resources (Lukula, 1993:6; Sunday Sketch, 1993). This decision was bitterly contested by some Ogoni elite in MOSOP, who upon losing to the radical faction resigned their membership of the executive, thus paving the way for Saro-Wiwa to become the president of MOSOP. The aftermath of this open split in the MOSOP only served to fuel bitterness, distrust and a struggle for power within the Ogoni elite, and strengthened the determination of the state and the oil multinationals to neutralise the Saro-

Wiwa faction of MOSOP. While the state relied on force, Shell combined a sophisticated PR campaign targeted at denying any responsibility for the Ogoni crisis, and demonising MOSOP, particularly its vocal advocate and Shell critic, Saro-Wiwa. Less obvious, but more dangerous, was Shell's provision of logistical support and arms for the Nigerian security forces operating in the Niger delta (Ake, 1996; Duodu, 1996; Ghazi and Duodu, 1996).

By July 1993, the tense situation had escalated with more protests and communal clashes involving the Ogoni and their neighbours; first the Andoni in July, the Okrika in December 1993, and then, the Ndoki, in April 1994 (Robinson, 1996; Tell, 1994; Douglas, 1994; Akanni, 1994; Rowell, 1996). The magnitude of the destruction of human life (over a thousand people killed) and property, and the sophisticated arms used on the Ogoni fuelled the suspicion that the attacks on them were part of an orchestrated plot by the state and Shell, to subvert MOSOP's agenda and sow confusion within the ranks of the Ogoni. They were not alone in the strong suspicion of federal government and Shell complicity in the large scale of the violence unleashed against the Ogoni. The mass suffering, displacement and killing of thousands of Ogoni, inflicted not just pain on the people, but was intended to demoralise and defeat their will to protest and resist. According to Claude Ake (1994a, 1994b) a highly respected political scientist and member of the peace committee set up by the River state government:

> As far as we could determine, there was nothing in the dispute in the sense of territory, fishing rights, access rights, discriminatory treatment, which are the normal causes of these communal clashes. One could not help getting the impression that there were broader forces which might have been interested in perhaps putting the Ogonis under pressure, probably to derail their agenda.

It was in this context of tension, war, confusion and intense suspicion that, exploiting a factional squabble within MOSOP, four pro-federal Ogoni elite suspected of being sell-outs to the state and Shell were tragically murdered in Giokoo by a mob on May 21, 1994. Some MOSOP leaders, and suspected youth activists, including MOSOP President Ken Saro-Wiwa were arrested a day after the murders, and finally arraigned before the Justice Auta Tribunal eight months later on charges of inciting the mob to murder the four Ogoni elite. In the absence of the MOSOP leaders, a systematic reign of terror was unleashed under the rubric of "wasting operations", and the quest of Okutimo to "sanitise" Ogoni, and "rewind them out of mobilisation" (Olukoya, 1994:23). As Okutimo boasted of his "rewinding" tactics in Ogoni to a group of Nigerian and foreign journalists (and which was later telecast on American television networks):

> I will just take some detachment of soldiers; they will stay at the four corners of the town. They have automatic rifles that sound as death...We shall surround the town at night...The machine gun with 500 rounds will open up and then we are throwing grenades that are making eekpuwaa...and they know I am around. What do you think the people are going to do? We have already put

roadblocks on the main road, we do not want anybody to start running...so the option we have made was that we should drive all the people into the bush with nothing except the pants and the wrapper they are using that night.

In a letter to the Nigerian Head of state General Sanni Abacha, the Ogoni Patriotic Union (OPU, 1994)), appealed to him to intervene and stop the systematic destruction of the Ogoni:

We, who are about to be killed, hereby appeal to your Excellency and fellow Nigerians in the name of God to please order the immediate end to the ongoing mass killings, looting, raping, and sacking of villages, in Ogoniland by Nigerian soldiers.

Describing the ordeal of the Ogoni in some detail, the OCU noted that "the soldiers and mobile policemen come in truck-loads in the dead of night shooting indiscriminately while the villagers flee into the bush. Once the villages are deserted the soldiers break into shops and homes, looting every thing they see including household appliances, clothes, foodstuff, domestic animals, drinks, drugs and provisions. Finally, the soldiers set fire on the homes looted". Many more Ogoni died, were detained, sustained injuries, or worse still were displaced, and forced into the bleak and uncertain life of becoming refugees. There was no let up in the full-scale war waged against the unarmed and defenceless Ogoni villagers in spite of their appeals to the federal government and the international community. As it was, their appeals merely strengthened the resolve of the state-oil alliance and their local allies in the delta to put a violent end to the "threat" posed by MOSOP and the highly mobilised popular forces of the Ogoni, "once and for all". This was also to serve, both as a means of beheading the Ogoni revolution, and as a deterrent to other groups planning to follow the Ogoni road. For the Ogoni, it strengthened the strongly held belief that they were being severely short-changed in the Nigerian nation-state project, and that they were right, and stood to gain everything by struggling for self-determination and the control of oil. As later events were to show, it was a most costly project for all the sides in the conflict. Most important of all, state militarisation of Ogoniland, failed to crush the spreading spirit of national resistance in the delta.

After a trial which fell far short of the international standards of fairness (Birnbaum, 1995; CLO, 1995), and in which the team of defence lawyers were forced to withdraw from appearing before the tribunal in the face of intimidation by security forces; on November 10, 1995 Ken Saro-Wiwa and eight other MOSOP members (Barinem Kiobel, John Kpunien, Baribor Bera, Saturday Dobee, Felix Nuate, Nordu Eawo, Paul Levura, and Daniel Gbokoo) were hanged in spite of local and international pleas for clemency. The hangings were met with shock, disbelief and then, anger. Claude Ake resigned in protest from the Steering Committee of the MNOC-funded Niger Delta Environmental Survey (NDES) (1995), amid announcements that 20 Ogoni youth had been charged for the same offence for which Ken and the others had been hanged. The timing of the hangings to coincide with the meeting of the Summit of Commonwealth Heads of State in Auckland, New Zealand, further worsened the global outrage that followed the hangings, and confirmed Nigeria's pariah status in the comity of nations. Nigeria was suspended from the Commonwealth, the European Union imposed sanctions on the Nigerian military, Canada broke off diplomatic relations with Nigeria, while the United Nations Human Rights Commission appointed a special rapporteur for Nigeria. Abacha spent virtually the rest of his reign, and committed a lot of resources towards, battling against the increasing isolation of Nigeria in diplomatic circles. The diplomatic siege on Nigeria did not ease until well after General Abacha's sudden death in June 1998.

If Abacha's calculation was that beheading MOSOP would intimidate other ethnic minority movements in the Niger delta into silence, it turned out to be a grossly mistaken gamble. Rather, what followed, was another change of form in the protest movement, the rise of the militant Ijaw (Ijo) movement, and an escalation in the intensity and frequency of the pan-delta quest to end "internal colonisation", personal rule, and the federal expropriation of the oil resources of the Niger delta.

Oil Minorities Movements of the Niger Delta: Patterns of Continuity and Transformation

While the oil minorities continued with a pattern of ethnic identity politics whose foundation had been laid as far back as the second decade of the 20th century, certain significant changes became evident after the onset of crisis and adjustment. While in the 1950s and 1960s, minority identity politics had been led by the elite, who either through social clubs, political parties or states creation movements worked through existing political structures to pursue their agenda of self-determination and local autonomy, the situation in the 1990s was different. The reasons for this are not difficult to fathom.

As noted earlier, there was significant frustration that the post-civil war federal unity project had excluded oil minorities from direct access to oil, and power at the centre. They also "lost out" in the creation of state exercises until the 1990s when Rivers was split in two (Rivers and Bayelsa states), South-Eastern in two (Cross River and Akwa Ibom states) and Bendel state in two (Edo and Delta states). But even when these states were created, the federal control of oil remained unchanged, and the deepening economic crisis made nonsense of the exercise in the face of the lack of development, the peculiar terrain, and the long years of deliberate neglect the Niger delta had suffered. Besides, the states creation exercise in the delta also created "new ethnic minorities" in the new states, and re-fuelled communal rivalries and conflict thus contributing to insecurity in the region.

The further alienation of the oil minorities by the federal state during the Babangida years confirmed their worst fears that the pact entered into with the federalist project during the civil war with the promise of reaping the full benefits of the oil resources of the delta (and oil boom), had been betrayed. This acted as a fillip for the re-assertion of oil minority ethnic identity, as a collective metaphor of the "victim", organising the masses to challenge the unitary federal state project (of the non-oil producing majority ethnic nationalities) that had fed fat on oil, while they the owners of the land, had nothing to show. The images of treachery, outsiders versus the owners of the land (oil), featured prominently in the quest of the oil minorities to challenge the legitimacy of the federal state, assert their local autonomy in order to control their resources, and force oil multinationals to respect the rights (and authority) of the people.

For so long, the people of the Niger delta had suffered in silence under the leadership of an elite which struggled to reproduce itself as a local ruling class through being co-opted by the federal state and oil multinationals operating in the oil producing communities, and serving as local gatekeepers. This faction of the oil minorities' elite co-opted by state and oil, which benefited from the spoils of oil in ways described earlier in this paper, has often used the anger and frustrations of the masses as a basis for bargaining with, and getting more state (and MNOC) patronage and largesse for themselves. They adopted an ambivalent strategy of appearing to carry the burden of the people's grievances as their representatives, and acting as the friends of the federal state and oil multinationals guaranteeing the co-operation of their people with the federal project, through promises and half-hearted gestures allegedly designed to address the complaints of the people.

This trend was replicated in their politics at the various levels and institutions of governance. In the politics of the Second Republic and the truncated Third Republic, the role of this elite in the mainstream political parties was at best ambiguous as it failed to push a broad-based agenda for the Niger delta, except in the race for office, contracts and state patronage. It is conceded that given the structure of the political parties, especially the government-sponsored Social Democratic Party and the National Republican Party of the Babangida years, and the militarisation of society, the elite had a difficult option of either committing "class suicide" or burrowing deeper into the federal project. Most chose the latter over the former, even if covertly. But as the oil revenues shrank further, and in the treacherous terrain of the Babangida and Abacha transitions, a lot of them lost out in the power game, joining the opposition either out of frustration, realisation that they had been used and dumped, or the fear of possible retribution being meted out to them by popular forces. The basis of their fears was real, for in the heat of the struggles in the delta, a lot of them were banished to the cities by the militant youth, and could not show their faces in their villages or communities where they were labelled as "sell-outs" (interviews during author's fieldwork, 1997–1999).

Others joined the opposition, for personal, sectional or worse still, treacherous reasons. Some also were faced with the dilemma of choosing between the high stakes of power (and bigger largesse available to those aligned to the state-oil alliance), and the high costs of being exposed to the people as a collaborator of an oppressive federal state with its exploitative foreign partners—the oil multinationals. This fractured elite was an explosive element in the Niger delta as they battled for the hearts and souls of the people of the Niger delta; a people battered by decades of oil extraction (and pollution), neglect, manipulation, and further ruined by years of crisis, adjustment, growing scarcities and repression. In contradistinction, the angry people emerged from their lethargy, and massed up behind the radical elite who had clearly embarked on a quest for self-determination based on a radical restructuring of Nigeria to give greater autonomy to ethnic constituents.

The escalation of tension, repression and conflict formed the volatile backdrop for the changing form of identity politics. Its hallmark was the decay of the elite-people coalition that had largely supported the post-civil war nation-state project. The emergence of a new coalition reflected the interests and aspirations of popular groups. Their loss of faith in existing national or formal local institutions led to the formation of mass-based oil minority identity-based associative groups. These "renewed" ethnic minority identity groups reflected a new bottom-up orientation in ethnic identity politics in the Niger delta. They mobilised the people at the grassroots to embark on mass demonstrations to protest state authoritarianism and block oil extraction as modalities of seeking redress, and power over oil. A significant development was the prominent role played by the youth in the struggle, and the implications of this generational shift in the power relations, in terms of the overall direction and form of identity politics in the delta.

As noted earlier, this associative movement of local resistance was neither homogenous, nor was its progress unilinear. What became clear from the early 1990s was that the struggles of the oil minorities movements had become one of the most advanced and complex forms of identity politics in Nigeria. The new ethnic movements in the delta succeeded in welding the grievances of the oil minorities onto the larger social concerns for democracy, equity and true federalism. Thus, they were able to connect the struggle at the national and global levels, in ways that were unprecedented in Nigeria's postcolonial history.

From the foregoing, it is possible to discern some of the most crucial aspects of the processes of decay and renewal in the oil minorities movement and locate them in some of the social contradictions reinforced by adjustment and authoritarianism in Nigeria. These processes were complex, while those of renewal responded as much to the past, as they did to the present. Historical and ethnic nationality icons, myths and culture were all pressed into service to construct an ethnic identity that rejected oppression, and yearned for social justice. Indeed, past struggles against the British and then the Nigerian state, heroes of self-determination, traditional symbols of solidarity, and national pride and the sacred ties between man, the land and water, were invoked, revived and integrated into local discourses of resistance and oil minority nationalism. All these were then merged with the openings offered by the changes at the domestic and global levels, to construct a potent force for the renewed struggles of the oil minorities of the Niger delta. For the people it was their collective survival and social justice that were at stake, and for the youth, it was the land and their tomorrow.

New Trends, New Contradictions in the Delta: Identity as National Liberation

An important aspect of the popularisation of the oil minorities movements in the Niger delta was the construction of indigenous collective symbols and metaphors for concretising their identities, and defining their mission. In the case of MOSOP, national pride founded on the non-defeat of the Ogoni in war before the coming of the British colonisers, their natural prowess as a people: farmers, fisher-people, hunters, traders and fierce warriors, were invoked in the course of the drawing up of the Ogoni Bill of Rights and the formation of MOSOP. This established grassroots support for the struggle for Ogoni self-determination, compensation for oil extraction and pollution; and the position that Ogoni control of its oil-rich territory was morally correct and just. The OBR (see Appendix 2) which was adopted by the Ogoni on August 26, 1990 and presented to the federal government on behalf on the Ogoni people by Ken Saro-Wiwa in his capacity as the president of the Ogoni Central Union, was debated at all levels of Ogoni society. Furthermore, to reinforce its legitimacy, the document was signed by the kings and representatives of five Ogoni kingdoms: Babbe, Gokanna, Ken-Khana, Nyo-Khanna, and Tai (Saro-Wiwa, 1995:70). These went a long way in building faith and confidence in the rightness of the MOSOP agenda, and inevitable victory of the Ogoni national project. Thus emboldening the people to confront the Nigerian state and Shell. To give flesh to the spirit of Ogoni nationalism, MOSOP had a flag, and a national anthem that summed up the nationalist aspirations and moral advantage of the Ogoni movement. Another movement, pan-delta in focus, the Chikoko draws its very name from the rich dark soils of the mangrove swamps of the delta.

The same trend of constructing indigenous symbols of collective identity is replicated in the Ijaw movement, which seeks to deconstruct the state boundaries balkanising the Ijaw between six states of the Nigerian federation. Although the revival of the pan-Ijaw movement was done by the Ijaw National Congress (INC), more militant and younger elements, the Ijaw Youth Council (IYC), have taken over the process at community level drawing on indigenous idioms to empower their struggle locally and projecting it globally. These Ijaw militants operate through organisations such as the IYC, NDVF, EBA and the INC. Like the Ogoni, the Ijaw have drawn up the Kaiama Declaration of December, 1998, which encapsulates the essence of Ijaw neo-nationalism, and was drawn up and approved by youth representatives from five hundred Ijaw communities (of over forty clans comprising the Ijaw ethnic nation) and 25 representative organisations.

Most critical of the recently popular Ijaw idioms are those of Egbesu and Ogele. Egbesu, is synonymous with truth and justice. As such it provides legitimacy for those fighting injustice and oppression. It is also interpreted to mean that with Egbesu on their side, the Ijaw are assured of winning. According to an Egbesu member, "the Egbesu is the unifying spirit of the Ijaw" (Guardian, 1998:19). According to Oronto Douglas in an interview (Olufemi and Don-Pedro, 1999):

> Egbesu, as I understand from our elders and respected Ijaw scholars, is one of the numerous traditional and cultural endowments among the Ijaw people. It is unique, in that it is closely associated with liberation and justice. You can say without fear of contradiction that Egbesu is also the god of war.

Indeed, there is a militant Ijaw youth movement led by Alex Preye called the Egbesu Boys of Africa (EBA), which is committed to the liberation of the Ijaw, and Ijaw claims to the control of Ijaw oil (Ollor-Obari, 1999a). Indeed, there are allegations that members of Egbesu swear oaths of allegiance to the Egbesu deity, and undergo certain rituals, which fortify them against bullets and assure them of victory in battle. This has been used to explain the daring and precision with which the Egbesu militants have launched some of their attacks, and co-ordinated the struggles in the delta. Ogele on the other hand, is the traditional celebration of life and solidarity in Ijaw tradition, using dance, procession and song (Ogele, 1999). It has been deployed in mobilising the people at the grassroots in the delta, and holding mass peaceful demonstrations against the government: federal and state; and the oil companies. Elements of folklore, myth, drama, philosophy and history, are undergoing transformation and re-interpretation as modalities for galvanising the people to shake off any lethargy, and stand up to fight for the survival of their ethnic "nation".

Closely related to the foregoing, is the adopting by minority groups in the delta of icons or heroes, based on their contributions to the emancipation of their people or nations in the past. Two personalities in the nationalist history of the delta aptly portray this trend. They are Paul Birabi and Isaac Adaka Boro. Birabi, is a revered figure in Ogoni history. He is credited as being the first Ogoni graduate (with a degree in Mathematics from Southampton University), who did a lot in encouraging many Ogoni young people to get an education, and a good start in life. He was a nationalist politician who was elected into the Eastern Nigerian House of Assembly, then made it all the way to the National House of Representatives in Lagos, and was part of the Nigerian delegation to the Constitutional Conference in London in 1953 (Saro-Wiwa, 1995:24).

Birabi is credited as being one of the founding fathers of modern Ogoni nationalism. After his death in 1953, a lot was done to preserve his memory, and realise his vision of a strong, united and proud Ogoni nation. The first secondary school in Ogoni was named after Birabi as a way of preserving the memory of his important contribution to the development of the Ogoni nation, while his tomb was regarded as a sacred place for renewing the spirit of the Ogoni nation. Saro-Wiwa (1995:121) recalls, that before the historic Ogoni demonstration marking the World Indigenous Peoples Day on January 4, 1993, involving over 300,000 Ogoni people, they visited Birabi's grave for prayers. Birabi's mentoring of young people, also went a long way in helping the marginalised Ogoni in producing an educated elite that could compete with other groups for access to power and resources in Nigeria. He was instrumental to the development of the Ogoni Central Union (OCU) and the Ogoni State Representative Assembly (OSRA) in the 1950s. Several of the Ogoni who later assumed prominence, and occupied positions in government, at the state and federal levels were either beneficiaries of Birabi's vision and generosity, or those of people inspired by Birabi's example. His name and memory were often invoked in the cause of Ogoni solidarity, and MOSOP construction of the Ogoni nation committed to the survival of the Ogoni as a distinct people.

Among the Ijaw, particularly the youth, the name Isaac Adaka Boro, invokes a lot of reverence. Boro, as mentioned earlier was the Ijaw radical and youthful militant nationalist who led his guerrilla Niger Delta Volunteer Force (NDVF) to create the Niger Delta Republic, without success, in 1966. For leading the first abortive attempt to secede from Nigeria Boro was tried and found guilty of treason. He was released after a change in government only to be martyred fighting on the federal side against Biafran claims to Ijaw land (oil). Some landmarks in Port Harcourt, the River state capital, were named after Boro as a way of preserving his memory, and recording his contribution to the development of the state. The ideals for which he fought, and later died for; the liberation of the Ijaw from their oppressors, the formation of an Ijaw nation (republic), and Ijaw control of oil (Kaemi, 1982), were revived by the Ijaw youth in mobilising the people around the memory of Boro, a hero of Ijaw resistance and nationalism. It is hardly surprising that one of the new militant Ijaw youth movements has adopted the name of Boro's Niger Delta Volunteer Force (NDVF) in identifying itself with Boro's brand of heroic Ijaw nationalism, and drawing inspiration from it to rescue the Ijaw nation from its oppressors, the federal government and the oil multinationals.

It is also very significant, that the pan-Ijaw youth agenda for national liberation—the Kaiama Declaration of December 11, 1998 (see Appendix 1), asserting Ijaw ownership of all land and natural resources (including mineral resources), declaring non-recognition of all undemocratic decrees that rob the Ijaw of the right of ownership and control of their resources, and demanding the immediate withdrawal from Ijawland of all military forces of occupation and oil companies by December 30, 1998—was drawn up by the All Ijaw Youth Congress in Kaiama—Isaac Adaka Boro's birthplace. It was at this meeting, that the arrowhead of Ijaw nationalism led by the youth and their allies, formed the Ijaw Youth Council (IYC), to "co-ordinate the struggle of Ijaw people for self-determination and social justice".

The new movements of the oil minorities operated on the basis of an agenda that had a clearly national and social character. These were well debated at the grassroots, were radical in orientation and were well-grounded in local discourses and popular forces. Their demands were well couched in the language, to borrow Apter's (1998:121) apt coinage, of "the political ecology of citizenship". In other words, as citizens of Nigeria, they were asserting their legitimate right to make demands and claims on the state, and the right to hold the state liable if it failed to respond to these demands and complaints. Beyond this, it implied that the Nigerian state had no right to claim their loyalty if it continued to exploit and repress them, and deny them their legitimate rights as citizens and oil producing minorities.

The demands of the oil minorities movements became codified for the first time, as Bills of Rights, Charters, Resolutions or Declarations directed at the federal government and the oil multinationals. The first and most famous of these was the Ogoni Bill of Rights drawn up by the Ogoni people in 1990. Many other movements have since followed the OBR example. Some of these include: the Charter of demands by the Movement for the Payment of Reparations to Ogbia (MORETO), the Ogba Charter, the Isoko Youth Charter (Why we struck), the Resolutions of the Urhobo Economic Summit, the Communiqué of the Itsekiri Patriots General Conference, the Aklaka Declaration of the Egi people; and the Kaiama Declaration and "Operation Climate Change" of the Ijaw Youth Council (IYC). In addition to these charters and bills, resolutions from important meetings of these movements constituted another platform for making of demands, serving notice and delivering ultimatums to the federal government and oil companies.

Apart from minority nationality movements, there also emerged within the associative movement in the Niger delta a strong human and environmental rights intervention. The approach of these groups has been that of the defence of human and environmental rights within the context of the delta. They do this through a number of ways: educating the people about their rights, empowering them to fight for their rights, informing Nigerians and the international community about the violation of rights in the delta, and exposing the perpetuators of these violations. Others include, documenting the role of the state and oil multinationals in the violation of rights, identifying the victims, and ramifications of such violations, providing basic assistance to empower the people economically, politically and socially, and documenting the deleterious impact of the oil industry on the fragile delta ecosystem. They are also involved in networking with local groups, donors and international NGOs interested in promoting human rights in the Niger delta.

These rights groups include the Environmental Rights Action (ERA), an affiliate of the Civil Liberties Organisation (CLO), the Niger Delta Human Environmental Rescue Organisation (ND-HERO), the Institute of Human Rights and Humanitarian Law (IHRHL), and Watch the Niger Delta (WAND). ERA for instance was among other things, involved in the collation and dissemination of information about the state of human and environmental rights in the Niger delta, the activities of Shell and other petroleum companies, and the human and environmental rights implications of the actions and inactions of the central and state governments in the Niger delta (Niger Delta Alert,

1997). Through these groups, their publications (books, newsletters, press releases, faxes and messages posted on the Internet and international campaigns), the world has come to be well educated on the poor state of human rights in the Niger delta. In a recent Human Rights Watch Publication (1999), The Price of Oil, based on research, visits, and an investigation of the human rights situation in the delta, it is noted inter alia, that:

> We found repeated incidents in which people were brutalised for attempting to raise grievances with the companies; in some cases security forces threatened, beat, and jailed members of community delegations even before they presented their cases. Such abuses often occurred on or adjacent to company property, or in the immediate aftermath of meetings between company officials and individual claimants or community representatives.

The activities of these human and environmental rights groups did not end in the area of rights advocacy and activism, they were also involved in natural resource management and community development issues in the local communities. Thus though they did not overly display an ethnic nationalist card, these groups were very important strategic allies of the oil minorities movement. They empowered the claims of the oil minorities, provided a rights platform which had international legitimacy and acceptability for them, and touched base with the local communities, becoming in the process a part of the organic whole that is the oil minorities movement. It is hardly surprising therefore, that most of these human rights activists are also in the forefront of the ethnic nationality movements in the delta.

The oil minorities groups were in themselves social coalitions which over time had evolved from an elite-led, top-bottom orientation, to one that had a broad social base with emphasis on popular representation of interest groups, and their full participation in the political and decision-making process. This pattern was played out in the processes that led to the drawing up of the OBR in 1990, and the formation of MOSOP the following year.

In the 1950s and 1960s Ogoni nationalism was projected by Ogoni Central Union (OCU), Ogoni State Representative Assembly (OSRA), and the Ogoni Divisional Union (ODU). The Ogoni Central Union remained active in the 1970s when some elite Ogoni social clubs were formed. The OCU was revived in the late 1980s, and was highly instrumental in the drawing up of the OBR in 1990, and the formation of MOSOP the following year. In the 1980s and 1990s, the prominent Ogoni elite clubs were the Ogoni Klub and Kagote Club, among others. It was partly out of the brainstorming of members of this Ogoni elite that the MOSOP idea was born. They were the ones that were to provide the leadership at the levels of the steering committee and executive committee of MOSOP. But most of the legwork and mobilisation at the grassroots was done by the Ogoni youth. They were the ones who welded the OBR onto local discourses and dialects, winning the villagers over, and heightening their faith in the possibility of realising Ogoni national autonomy and control of oil.

Thus, when MOSOP was finally born, it was more of an umbrella organisation of the various Ogoni interest groups: Federation of Women Associations (FOWA), National Youth Council of Ogoni People (NYCOP), Council of Ogoni Churches (COC), Council of Ogoni Professionals (COP), Council of Ogoni Traditional Rulers (COTRA), National Union of Ogoni Students (NUOS), Ogoni Students Union (OSU), Ogoni Teachers Union (OTU) and the Ogoni Central Union (OCU) (Barikor-Wiwa, 1997:46). That Ogoni traditional rulers and elite actively supported the OBR and MOSOP was evidence of the broad social consensus that underscored the MOSOP agenda. Particularly strategic for the popular forces was that MOSOP provided a platform to voice their grievances and exercise power for the first time, for the elite, it was a more sophisticated platform to pursue their own agenda.

In the popularisation of oil minorities movements, it is possible to discern two critical developments: a generational shift in power towards the youth and the subsequent decline in the moral authority and influence of the gerontocrats; and a more prominent gender profile for women's groups in the dialectics of the struggle. As has been noted with regard to MOSOP (NYCOP) and the IYC and Chikoko, the youth played very critical roles in defining the struggles in new national and social terms, organised and mobilised the people for action, thus effectively controlling the social agenda for change at the grassroots. They were the foot-soldiers, who organised and led the various acts of protest and local resistance, offering themselves at the most as an alternative radical leadership to the oil minorities movements, or at the very least, as a potent restraining force on the excesses, opportunism and greed of the elders and the "colluding" elite.

In the case of the "popularisation" of MOSOP the militant NYCOP elements played a critical role in the everyday politics, and in purging the leadership of MOSOP of those it considered as traitors—usually the conservative elders or moderate elite who were worried that the movement was moving too fast and endangering their own political ambitions at the federal level (within the context of the Babangida and Abacha transitions). These conservatives were alarmed at a trend they interpreted as the personalisation of the MOSOP agenda by Ken Saro-Wiwa and his radical supporters, particularly the NYCOP militants, who they branded Saro-Wiwa's private army and a weapon for intimidating and even killing his enemies (Ogoni Study Group, n.d; Orage, 1998). They were particularly miffed by the way that Saro-Wiwa and his supporters took over the MOSOP decision-making platform in a manner reminiscent of democratic centralism. Thus Dr Leton (President) and Chief Kobani (Vice-President) resigned their positions in the MOSOP executive, paving the way for Saro-Wiwa to become the President of MOSOP, with Ledum Mitee, a lawyer and human rights activist as the Vice-President. In a bid to fight against their displacement from the mainstream of Ogoni politics, the conservatives led by Dr Garrick Leton, Albert Badey, Dr Kenneth Birabi Edward Kobani and Chief Orage strengthened their alliance with the state and global oil, first to settle scores with the radicals, especially their leader,

Ken Saro-Wiwa, and expose them as agitators bent on causing trouble for the federal government and oil companies, and misrepresenting the peace-loving and loyal Ogoni people. This led to a strong response from Ken Saro-Wiwa, the radicals and militants who exploited the fact that they controlled power at the grassroots to label the conservatives, "vultures"—as the enemies of the Ogoni who collaborated with outsiders to exploit (prey upon) their own people. Lacking a strong social base the conservatives were driven to desperation, while the radicals were driven by unprecedented popular power and support from the "global" civil society. It was in the middle of this zero-sum factional struggle for power, oil and control of MOSOP within the Ogoni elite versus the forces of the status quo and those of change, that the four Ogoni chiefs (Edward Kobani, Albert Badey, Samuel Orage and Theophilus Orage) were brutally murdered, and the globalised forces of extraction moved in, in an attempt to finish off the Ogoni revolution. It is thus hardly surprising that after the "Ogoni nine" were hanged, twenty youth were lined up before the tribunal for the same treatment only to be saved by local and international pressures and Abacha's death in June 1998.

The same trend of inter-generational tensions can be seen in the interactions between the elders of the Ijaw National Congress (INC), and the Youth of the Ijaw Youth Congress (IYC). While the INC is basically moderate or even conservative, the IYC is radical and critical of the INC, rejecting in some cases, agreements made by the INC with the federal government on behalf of the Ijaw nation. For instance, while Ijaw elders have appealed to the youth to postpone "Operation Climate Change" intended to shut down all oil installations in Ijawland if the MNOCs failed to respond to the Kaiama Declaration; the IYC has turned down the request (Ollor-Obari, 1999c). The current tussle between the elders in the Isoko Development Union (IDU) and the Isoko National Youth Forum (INYF), typifies the recent trend of inter-generational wars in the delta. In December 1998 the INYF had forcefully shut down Shell oil flow stations at Olomoro-Oleh, Oroni (Igbide), Uzere, Ogini and Otoro-Owhe, in protest against Shell neglect and marginalisation (Ezomon, 1999b:24–26). The elders in the IDU after consultations with Shell officials and those of a Delta state government delegation invited Shell to resume its operations, only for the INYF to re-impose its siege on the flow stations on January 12, 1999, on the grounds that "the elders had breached the confidence of the youth by inviting Shell to resume work, without the youths' consent". It was not until the youth were consulted by the IDU that the siege was suspended under certain conditions (Okafor, 1999a). In a region where respect for age and seniority has from earliest times been an important aspect of indigenous culture and tradition, the ascendancy of youth power does not merely interrogate the basis of traditional power, authority and control, it feeds into the existing revolutionary tensions and pressures from below ravaging the Niger delta.

The reasons for the rise of the youth are not difficult to fathom, and are tied to the fact that they are the ones who stand to lose the most if the status quo of exploitation, pollution, repression and marginalisation persists in the Niger delta. Most of the youth though educated, with high school diplomas and university degrees are unemployed. Those without education are worse off, there is little land to farm, fishing requires a heavy capital outlay and is very expensive and difficult considering the rate of oil spills in the delta. Fisher people have to travel far out to the sea for their catch, or along rivers and ponds unaffected by spills, all requiring strong and expensive motor boats, and fuel (resulting from years of the devaluation of the Naira and removals of petroleum subsidy) which is scarce and very costly in the Niger delta. Under these conditions, there is little else to do except drift towards "benefit capture" or insecure menial jobs as labourers in the oil industry. Under the condition of grinding poverty in the oil producing communities of the Niger delta, placed side by side with the opulence and high standard of living of the oil workers, expatriate and Nigerian, there has been a lot of resentment. This fed into the unfulfilled expectations and anger of the delta youth.

The youth under crisis and adjustment never had the relatively privileged status of those who graduated during the oil boom years; they are therefore hungry, angry and frustrated. They have lost confidence in the traditional rulers, elders and colluding elite who have over time, conspired with the state and oil multinationals to act as gatekeepers while their own people suffered. The predatory instincts of the Nigerian elite and the nature of oil as a wasting asset further fuelled their desperation. As the case of Oloibiri, Nigeria's oldest oil well, which was abandoned after the oil flow stopped, showed, the youth calculated that once the oil in the delta was totally sucked out and dried up, the oil multinationals would move out, and they would be abandoned to a bleak future in a neglected and wasted land. As such, they are determined to strike before it becomes too late, and salvage their today so as not to lose their tomorrow. The youth are angry and desperate, and the elders, mostly compromised and having very little moral authority, are giving way to the raw energy and radical militancy of younger elements in the struggle for self-determination. Yet, the elders and elite (and their backers) are not giving up the power and privileges they have accumulated as gatekeepers, and the very basis of their survival as a local ruling class; without giving the youth a good fight, thus contributing to the escalating tension in the delta. Yet, on a general note, the youth have become a most potent force in the popularisation of identity politics in the Niger delta force, and in raising the effectiveness of the protests of the oil minorities and their blocking power.

Closely related to the foregoing is the greater role being played by women's groups in the oil minorities movements. A closer scrutiny of MOSOP's struggles and the on-going one of the IYC, vividly reveal the role of women in the struggles for self-determination in the Niger delta (Barikor-Wiwa, 1996; Obi, 1998d; ND-HERO, 1998a; Obibi, 1999a; Ogele, 1999). With respect to MOSOP, the Federation of Ogoni Women (FOWA), played a very important role in sensitising women to the importance of organising themselves to support the OBR and work towards the success of the MOSOP agenda. Ogoni women participated in demonstrations against Shell and the state, bore enormous sacrifices, when their sons, husbands and fathers were shot or arrested, when they themselves were arrested, their homes invaded by Nigerian soldiers, who looted, beat and raped them (CLO, 1996; ERA, 1996). A lot of Ogoni women lost their lives in the communal clashes involving the Ogoni and their neighbours between 1993 and 1994. Similarly, they were forced to live in the bush for long periods or ended up in refugee camps outside the country. FOWA played an important role in getting relief materials and medicines for Ogoni refugees and those displaced (Barikor-Wiwa, 1996), co-ordinating fact-finding tours by western NGOs in the delta, and promoting the Ogoni cause, locally and globally. FOWA opened up offices in North America and Europe from where it contributed to the struggle at home. In the same way, the Ijaw National Alliance has been operating from the United States in globalising the cause of Ijaw nationalism, and publicising the violation of rights of rights in the Niger delta by the state-oil alliance.

Any treatment of the on-going struggles of the Ijaw ethnic nationality of the Niger delta would be incomplete without the inclusion of the role of the Niger Delta Women for Justice (NDWJ). The NDWJ supported the Kaiama Declaration of December 11, 1998 and the youth agenda for Ijaw self-determination. On January 11, 1999 the NDWJ mobilised thousands of women to Port Harcourt, at grave risk, to protest the shooting of Ijaw youth during an Ogele procession in front of the Bayelsa state governor's office, and ask the government to enter into dialogue with the Ijaw (Obibi, 1999a:1–2). According to Aniemeseigha Brisibe of the NDWJ:

> We cannot afford to fold our hands and watch our sons killed our women raped and our lands polluted by the oil companies. As mothers, sisters, and daughters of Ijawland, we are the sanctuaries of continuity (Ogele, 1999:1).

Another important trend is the proliferation of oil minorities movements in the Niger delta since the late 1980s (Obi, 1995, 1998a, 1999). Rather than be crushed by state repression, the groups have been springing up like mushrooms after the rains. After the Ogoni hangings in 1995, the groups have not only multiplied; they have become more militant and sophisticated in their approach. More recently, however, there have been attempts to bring them together such as the Chikoko, which was launched at Aleibiri in Bayelsa state on August 17, 1997, or at least to get them to work together.

Equally interesting is the emergence of charismatic, radical individuals in the leadership of most popular minority movements in the Niger delta. In a way, it echoes the heroism of the Boros and Birabis of the Niger delta, and fits into the quest of the people for a new Moses who would lead them to the promised land where they would be free from their oppressors and control their oil. Individuals like Ken Saro-Wiwa (MOSOP), Oronto Douglas, Felix Tuodolo, Tim Kaiser-Wilhem Ogoriba, Isaac Osuoka, Kingley Kuku and Alex Preye (IYC) are emerging as the present-day heroes of the oil minorities movement. Their heroism has to a large extent been tied to the way they have turned to the past to re-interpret the present, reinforce "moral ethnicity" (Londsdale, 1996:131), and provide an alternative vision of a future delta society based on the principles of truth, justice, equity and a great faith in carrying the people along. They were able to do this, basically by operating within associative movements, and demonstrating a strong commitment to the course of the people. In a region where most of the elite and elders had already been compromised by their opportunism, and the gatekeeper nexus, the new radical leadership easily won a large following among the majority of the people.

Table 4. *Major oil minority movements in the Niger delta since 1990*

Movement for the Survival of Ogoni People (MOSOP)
Ijaw National Congress (INC)
Ijaw Council for Human Rights (ICHR)
Council for Ikwerre Nationality
Ethnic Minority Rights Organisation of Africa (EMIROAF)
Southern Minorities Movement (SMM)
Movement for the Payments of Reparations to Ogbia (MORETO)
Federated Niger Delta Ijaw Community,
Ijaw Peace Movement (IPM)
Ijaw Youth Council (IYC)
Ijaw Elders Forum (IEF)
Itsekiri Nationality Patriots
Chikoko
Egbesu Boys of Africa (EBA)
Niger Delta Women for Justice (NDWJ)
Bayelsa Forum
Movement for the Survival of the Ijaw Ethnic Nationality in the Niger Delta (MOSIEND)
Isoko Development Union
Isoko National Youth Movement (INYM)
Egi Women's Movement (EWM)
Egi National Congress (ENC)
Ogba Solidarity
Traditional Rulers of Oil Mineral Producing Areas of Nigeria (TROMPCON)
Urhobo Progressive Union
Urhobo Study Group
Rivers Coalition

Source: Author's fieldwork and Nigerian newspapers.

These groups are now reaching out to other ethnic nationality and human rights groups outside the Niger delta in rejecting the "new" transition and insisting on a Sovereign National Conference of all ethnic nationalities and interest groups in Nigeria to debate, and decide how best to tackle the national question, and restructure the Nigerian federation.

Apart from its links with ERA, and CLO, IYC has been reaching out to MOSOP, the Yoruba nationality movement—the O'Odua Peoples' Congress (OPC), the Southern Minorities Movement, the Egi Women's Movement, and the oil labour unions: the National Union for Petroleum and Natural Gas Workers (NUPENG) and the Petroleum and Natural Gas Senior Staff Association of Nigeria (PENGASSAN). It is clear that just as the social base of the struggle is being broadened in the delta, the movements are now expanding through networking with other aggrieved nationalities and civil society groups outside the delta, to construct a national platform for the struggle for true federalism and democracy in Nigeria.

Regarding the very nature of oil minorities movements in the Niger delta, they are becoming increasingly militant in their approach to the volatile politics in their region (Agidee, 1999; Obibi, 1999c; Ofuoku, 1998; Ollor-Obari, 1999e; Ezomon, 1999b). The basic strategies remain the use of revolutionary pressures and popular blocking power to force the federal government, oil multinationals and the local colluding elite to attend to their demands. This has impacted adversely on the rate of extraction and accumulation of oil-based capital by global oil, to the growing alarm of local gatekeepers and wariness of the officials of oil multinationals and their home-governments. More recently other parties, including western diplomats and "goodwill ambassadors" such as Reverend Jesse Jackson and Jimmy Carter have had some dialogue with some of these movements. It has become clear to all the forces on the ground in the delta, that since the 1995 hangings, things can no longer be done in the old way. Rather then rely on passive resistance or a strictly non-violent approach (as in the case of MOSOP), the movements have become not merely protest movements, but militant resistance movements, expressing their grievances, but also defending themselves by offensive means (Obibi, 1999b, 1999c; Ofuoku, 1999).

The radical wing of the movements has demonstrated increased blocking power, stopping oil production in several parts of the Niger delta in 1998, and reducing Nigeria's oil production to its lowest level since 1995 (EIU, 1999:28). It is clear that they have not been intimidated by the "Ogoni example", and have rather stepped up the intensity of the struggle based on lessons learnt from the MOSOP revolution. As a report by Onanuga, in *The News* magazine (1998:13), shows, the first half of 1998 marked a high point in the struggle for the Niger delta:

> ... Between January and August this year, Shell recorded 55 attacks on its installations and equipment loss of close to N51 billion. Total work days lost as a result of work stoppage are estimated at 103 days.

Painting a grim picture of the impact of the revolutionary pressures in the Niger delta on oil production and accumulation, the EIU Country Report (Nigeria) for the last quarter of 1998 notes, that:

In a concerted onslaught at the beginning of October Ijaw youth attacked oil installations belonging to the Anglo-Dutch Company Shell, the Italy-based Agip and the US-based Chevron. For much of the month production was cut by 610,000 barrels per day (b/d), some 28% of the country's output. Armed protesters occupied 15 flow stations, cutting 378,000 b/d of crude feeding Shell's Forcados and Bonny oil terminals. They attacked Agip's pipeline, forcing it to suspend loading at its 130,000 b/d Brass River terminal. Ijaw youths also temporarily seized six flow stations belonging to Chevron, resulting in losses of up to 105,000 b/d.

Under increased pressures from Ijaw, and Isoko youth that had blocked its oil installations in parts of the delta, Shell was compelled to declare a force majeure on January 16, 1999, suspending oil exports at its Bonny and Forcados oil terminals, as at that time, "ten of its flow stations were occupied, and Isoko youth had seized an additional five flow stations, while a spill in the Santa Barbara river had forced the company to shut down five flow stations with an estimated capacity of 145,000 b/d" (EIU Report, 1999:28). While giving a distorted image of the crisis in the Niger delta from the view of the oil multinationals, the EIU report fails to draw attention to the role of these companies in the escalation of the conflict in the delta through decades of exploitation, pollution, intimidation, corruption and collusion with the military to violently repress the rights of the people. Yet, it does show an acknowledgement of the blocking power of the youth on oil-based accumulation in Nigeria.

The response of the state and the oil multinationals to the increased militarisation of the oil minorities movement has remained ambivalent, relying on a mixture of organised violence, and the exploitation of divisions within the ranks of the movements. One thing remains clear, the forces which have monopolised the oil resources of the Niger delta are determined to defend their power over oil at any cost, while those seeking to break this monopoly and the centralised socio-political system that sustains it, are equally determined to do so any cost.

After the December 11, 1998 Kaiama declaration by the Ijaw Youth, the struggle in the delta assumed a more dangerous dimension in the midst of the mobilisation of people and troops throughout the delta. In places like Ogbia, Bomadi, Kaiama, Oloibiri, the site of Nigeria's first oil well, and Yenagoa, the Bayelsa state capital, the youth held Ogele rallies and reinstated their support for the cause of the Ijaw nation and solidarity with the Kaiama declaration. On December 30, a day to the expiration of the ultimatum given to oil companies to leave Ijawland, a state of emergency was declared throughout Bayelsa state by its military administrator, Lt-Col Edo Obi (Reuters, 1998). That same day, twenty six Ijaw youth participating in an Ogele demonstration near the administrator's office were reportedly shot dead (Ollor-Obari and Ezomon, 1999:1–2; Project Underground, 1999; INC-USA, 1999a; ND-HERO, 1998b; Ollor-Obari, 1998f)).

Thousands of fully armed, battle-ready troops of the Nigerian army were mobilised throughout Yenagoa and other parts of Bayelsa state. They were to be followed by Navy gunboats, before fanning out across the villages in Bayelsa, Delta and Rivers states (Ollor-Obari, 1999:f 1–2) ostensibly to protect oil installations. Oil installations were placed under military guard in the unprecedented militarisation of Bayelsa state. Since the end of the Nigerian civil war, this was the first time a state of emergency was being declared in the Niger delta, and the Navy (Navy Special Security Task Force) directly involved in an operation of this kind. But it did underscore the desperation of the centralist forces to defend their monopoly of oil. A reign of terror was unleashed in the creeks, swamps and villages of Ijawland, with the centres of the Ogele being marked for "special treatment" by the military. Lives were lost, many people were injured, displaced, houses were burnt and many people were arrested or threatened (Ikwenze, 1999; Ollor-Obari, 1999a, 1999b). Soldiers moved into Kaiama—the historical site of Ijaw resistance and nationalism—sacking the town over confusing reports of an earlier attack on Nigerian troops by the Egbesu Boys, and the holding of an Ogele in defiance of the state of emergency declared by the state administrator. The leadership of the IYC and the EBA went underground but many of them, including the president of the MOSIEND, T K Ogoriba one of the signatories of the Kaiama declaration, were arrested and placed in detention. Events in Ijawland since December have been reported across the world.

In the 1999 budget speech, the Nigerian head of state, General Abdulsalami Abubakar, warned the delta youth to stop holding the nation to ransom, even while acknowledging that their grievances were genuine (National Concord, 1999:1–2; Esajere, 1999:1–2). Reading the "riot act" to the oil minorities' forces, the newspapers further quoted from General Abubakar's budget speech:

> ... Genuine as these grievances may be, we cannot allow the continued reckless expression of such feelings...Disruptions of the activities of oil companies, government and private enterprises by rampaging youth, seizure of oil wells, rigs and platforms as well as hostage-taking and vehicular-hijacking are totally unacceptable to this administration. We will not accept brazen challenge to the state authority under threat of violence as happened recently in the Niger Delta region.

This warning underscored the zero-sum approach to oil politics, and the fact that the "monopolist" state (and global oil capital) would view any challenge to its hold over the oil wells—its very lifeblood—as a threat to its own life, treason, to be punished by death. It is from this perspective, that Abubakar's warning can be viewed, vis à vis the contending claims of the oil minorities. The delta has remained under heavy military occupation in spite of the protests of the people. While the troops were still holding onto the delta, selected indigenes of the Niger delta were invited to Abuja to dialogue with the head of state. It is significant that the youth were not among those invited. Meanwhile, the federal government went ahead to announce a 15.3 billion Naira development plan for the Niger delta, and then set up yet another panel, headed by General Oladayo Popoola to look into the problems of the Niger delta. The Popoola-led Presidential Committee on Development Options for the Niger Delta was made up of military officers, and Popoola himself a non-indigene of the delta is a top military officer and an appointee of the federal government. It is therefore no surprise that the oil minorities have rejected the recommendations of the Popoola-led panel (Olufemi, 1999; Ollor-Obari, 1999g, Ollor-Obari and Okafor, 1999).

This is largely a repeat of the usual federal approach to the minority question in the delta. The people are excluded from the processes, from the consultation and decision-making, and their rights are subordinated to the extractive politics and greed of the ruling class, the oil multinationals, and the "colluding" elite of the Niger delta. Even moderate groups like INC are being sidelined by the federal government, which prefers to deal with individuals, rather than groups. Under the guise of spending money on the delta's problems, billions have gone, and still go to the gatekeepers in the delta, and their federal patrons, but these huge sums hardly ever address the real problems in the oil producing communities. It is therefore not surprising that side by side with the announcement of the release of billions of Naira for development in the delta, the setting up of a high-powered federal panel to oversee the process, and the revival of OMPADEC, under a new board and chief executive, armed troops continue to occupy the region, unleashing mayhem on hapless villagers, and protesting youth who are increasingly resorting to guerrilla war tactics.

Since January 1999, there has been another upsurge in military activity against protesting villagers. In most of these cases of repression in the Niger delta, the oil multinationals have continued to been directly or indirectly implicated (Human Rights Watch, 1999). This is in the form of inviting security forces to protect oil installations from rampaging villagers, to intimidate and arrest those individuals leading community protests or claims for compensation, or exploiting existing cleavages to instigate intra- or inter-communal conflict and confusion. In the midst of all the confusion, conflict and destruction, the MNOCs continue to milk the delta of its oil, under military protection. They invite, sustain, and supply some intelligence and logistical support as well as other "sweeteners" to the armed soldiers who wage war on the people for daring to challenge the companies and the federal government. Specifically Shell, Chevron and Agip have been involved in the latest incidents in the delta. In April 1999, a community, the Ekebiri community, in Bayelsa state, demonstrated against the Nigerian Agip Oil Company (NAOC). The bone of contention was a claim of 12 million Naira made on the company by the Ekebiri community, as compensation for frequent oil spillage between 1979–1997, and which Agip had refused to pay. By April 17, the talks had become deadlocked, and the community forcibly shut down Agip installations, which Agip officials under military escort forcibly reopened the following day. That same day, the Ekebiri youth re-took the installations and shut them down again. Agip returned with more armed soldiers and they opened fire on two boats suspected of carrying Ekebiri activists. According to some reports, between 2 and 8 youth were killed, many injured, and arrested, while the village of Ekebiri was sacked (ND-HERO, 1999; Obibi, 1999c:2).

In the case of Chevron, the company has used its boats and helicopter to ferry armed soldiers to attack and kill protesting villagers in the Niger delta. The shooting of two youths on Chevron's Parabe platform off the coast of Ondo state by security forces transported by Chevron in May 1998, in a bid to dislodge protesters who had shut down production (Human Rights Watch, 1999:12) and shootings in some Ijaw host-communities in 1999, typify the modalities through which global oil protects its investments in the delta. According to Amy Goodman, an American radio journalist who visited Nigeria in 1998, to investigate conflict between Ilaje youth and Chevron (at Parabe), an unnamed Chevron official admitted "that the oil company transported the troops to the (oil) platform by helicopter", the argument being that, "as a foreign company, it must obey the dictates of Nigeria's ruling generals and cannot stop the regime from using company aircraft and helicopter for military purposes" (cited in Akande, 1999). Chevron's cynicism and culpability was further betrayed, when its parent company in the United States banned the American radio station that broadcast Amy's reports (Pacifica) for the "bad press" the exposé gave Chevron as a collaborator of the military in repression of Nigerians in the delta. The recent reports of Agip-backed and Elf-instigated attacks on oil communities in the delta similarly fit into the pattern of MNOC-State repression (ND-HERO, 1999). The state-MNOC alliance has therefore tightened its control over oil by violent means. Their partnership clearly transcends joint-ventures in exploration, production and extraction of oil, but also includes the dictatorship of the oil monopolists ready to defend their control of oil at any cost.

The rising violence in the delta is clearly a disturbing trend. The upsurge in violence in the form of communal clashes involving armed youth, kidnappings, car jacking and the taking of expatriate staff of oil companies hostage by armed gangs or protesting communities, or in the form of military reprisals, aided by oil multinationals, against protesting oil communities, is an ill-wind that can easily grow into a whirlwind. Unfortunately, the stakes are so high, and rigid positions taken on all sides that given the zero-sum approach adopted so far, violence will continue to exact a great toll on the delta, until the fundamental grievances of the people are fairly addressed, and the contradictions within the oil minorities movements themselves are resolved.

It remains clear that the central issue of control is still being hotly contested. The federal government deliberately continues to ignore the demands for a transfer of control over oil, while bigger tokens are being dangled before the eyes of the oil minorities' elite, who are themselves, caught in the horns of a dilemma. If they "eat", they are damned in the eyes of the masses, who have been paying a high price for resisting expropriation; if they do not "eat", they are equally damned in the eyes of the federal government and oil multinationals, who have provided them with largesse as reward for their "loyalty".

The other side of the coin is repression and what Admiral Akhigbe, when he was then Chief of Naval Staff, was said to have referred to as the "physical thrust of force", the use of military force as an appropriate response to oil community unrest in the Niger delta (INC, 1999:22). Dialogue between the federal government and the oil minorities movements has therefore been structured out of the process, so that the issue of re-negotiating the control of oil cannot feature on the agenda, or the monopolisation of oil accumulation to the exclusion of the oil minorities, interrogated. The rising anger in the Niger delta cauldron is increasingly and steadily boiling over, thus, making this unresolved crisis a most explosive problem, and challenge for the incoming civilian administration of General Olusegun Obasanjo (retired).

The Globalisation of Local Struggles in the Niger Delta (1991–1999)

A significant development in the identity politics of the oil minorities movement is the development of the capacity to globalise the local struggles in the delta. This is hinged on a correct reading of changes at the global level and how local struggles can be empowered by tapping into the "global" and adopting its platform and discourse (Obi, 1998a; INC-USA, 1998; Ollor-Obari, 1999g, 1999h, 1999i). No doubt the growth in awareness and organising power of the oil minorities has been the result of their cumulative and collective experience, and the emergence of a younger alternate elite keen on changing the course of history. The recognition that the struggle could be waged at two levels, the local and the global, marked a clear advance in the dialectics of identity politics in the Niger delta. It also marked the clear recognition that local struggles were equally relevant to the unfolding realities of international relations in a globalising world.

Beyond the notion that it was operating through the adoption of "eco-politics as a critique of rentier capitalism" (Apter, 1998:153), the changing form of identity politics was therefore in part, a reaction to the contradictions arising from the deepening of globalised market relations in the delta. It was also in part a reaction to authoritarian relations in the delta: rising alienation and poverty, and intensified exploitation by oil multinationals. Therefore it was not surprising that given the local conditions in the Niger delta and Nigeria as a whole, and given the type of new leadership thrown up by the resurgence of ethnic minority movements, the ramifications of the struggle would transcend the local and connect to the global level. This was born out of the recognition by this new leadership, that as a function of capitalist (oil) accumulation, and as a repressive force, the "unequal partnership" between the Nigerian state and oil multinationals is mutually self-reinforcing. And that to strike at the heart of global oil, it must be exposed in its own backyard in Europe and North America, and global fora, as a violator of human rights in, and a reckless polluter of the Niger delta. In other words, for the struggle to be more effective, it had to transcend the localised terrain by appealing to and connecting to sympathetic global forces.

In a broad sense, the globalisation of struggles in the Niger delta pitched those forces acting at the behest of globalised oil accumulation versus those resisting it. This placed the Nigerian state and oil multinationals on a collision course with the oil minorities. The earliest group to globalise the local struggle in the Niger delta was the Movement for the Survival of Ogoni People (MOSOP). Rather than MOSOP simply and opportunistically latching onto a more liberalised post-cold war global order, it creatively devised strategies, and made immense sacrifices to pioneer globalised oil minority resistance. At the heart of its strategy was the making of the plight of the Ogoni in the hands of Shell and the Nigerian (military) state a major global issue. MOSOP also empowered its local claims through networking with western environmental and rights NGOs to form a global front against the extractive and repressive activities of Shell and the Nigerian state. To a large extent, MOSOP's success could be measured in terms of its capacity to use the platform of a global idiom of rights to push its local agenda. Two questions are apposite here. Why did the Ogoni target Shell in their quest to globalise the struggle for self-determination? How did the Ogoni connect to the global in building networks of resistance against globalised oil capital?

MOSOP's targeting of Shell is connected to Shell's prominent profile as one of the biggest and richest oil multinationals in the world, and the oldest (operating since 1938), biggest, richest and most visible oil operator in the Niger delta. Shell's position in global accumulation, and the fact that the Niger delta accounted for about 14 per cent of Shell's global oil production, and 51 per cent of Nigeria's oil production meant that the company was critical to the reproduction and domestication of capitalist relations in the Niger delta, and Nigeria. Beyond the delta, Shell was a source of good profits to shareholders in the industrial North, provided lots of jobs, and most important of all, was a critical supplier of the cheap energy needs of the G-7 countries.

It was therefore obvious that anyone who sought to confront Shell would of necessity need to come to terms with its national and global interface. Shell's contribution to Nigeria's state revenues (almost 50%), meant that the company had a lot of leverage with the federal government and in a sense Shell had "privatised2 the state, "operating under the umbrella of a repressive apparatus" (Ake, 1996). It was again clear that to confront the state, Shell was a relevant factor as the partner and benefactor of the extractive state. At the immediate locality of the delta, fifty years of Shell's presence had made it a domesticated player, a conquistador of sorts, which not only controlled the oil, land and waters of the people. Shell also intervened through the standard divide and rule tactics in local governance as: benefactor, extractor and tormentor. It was obvious that any agenda for the liberation of the delta had to begin with the challenge to the reign of the localised global oil conquistador, Shell.

MOSOP's resistance to global oil was therefore a sophisticated struggle for self-determination, adopting local empowerment, and the global medium of rights struggle. As noted elsewhere (Obi, 1998a):

> The insertion of the Ogoni resistance into the global rights agenda, its success in waging one of the most sophisticated environmental rights struggles in the 1990s was predicated not merely on the co-optation of the global rights discourse on the universalisation of human rights and freedom, but also, on a solid project of local popular empowerment and mass mobilisation, under a conscious leadership. This social force of the Ogoni, empowered the case made through, and in, the global rights discourses and won the attention and support of significant sections of global civil society to the cause of local resistance. Through MOSOP, global discourses were welded onto local identity, culture,

economy, and the quest for freedom. Ethnic identity became the metaphor for the rights struggle.

The formation of MOSOP was the culmination of the historical experience of the Ogoni as a minority people and victims of discrimination even within the delta. Through its strategy of local empowerment, it was able to transcend the limitations of its small size (500,000), and grab global attention. Local empowerment involved the popularisation of the Ogoni movement between 1990–1993 by MOSOP and its affiliate bodies, the drawing up of the OBR in 1990, and its addendum in 1991, and the decision after consulting the Ogoni people to appeal to the international community. This was after Shell and the state had ignored MOSOP's demands. Indeed, the issue went beyond the fact that for the first time many Ogoni were taking part in taking decisions affecting them as a people. It was that for the first time, they realised and used their blocking power against a powerful global actor like Shell and coercive apparatus of the Nigerian state without being intimidated. The Ogoni people rediscovered their power. Mass support, popular leadership and mobilisation were the key to the MOSOP revolution.

During the struggle, the Ogoni demonstrated their solidarity with MOSOP as the representative of the Ogoni people. The arrests of MOSOP leaders were protested loudly, and through demonstrations, and ultimatums given to oil multinationals were followed by mass action. In seeking to raise funds for the struggle the MOSOP set up the One Naira Survival Fund (ONESUF), in which a total sum of N700,000, at the rate of one Naira per head for every Ogoni, was raised. Later in the year, MOSOP set up the Ogoni Relief and Rehabilitation Fund (ORAREF), to take care of the Ogoni victims of military repression, or those who had been injured or displaced as a result of the "communal" clashes between the Ogoni and their neighbours between 1993–1994. Even when the repression of the MOSOP revolution was at its very worst, MOSOP helped its cadres and other Ogoni in gaining asylum in safe havens abroad. There was faith in the popular leadership of MOSOP as one that could deliver to the people, and not one that was greedy, treacherous and self-serving. In the euphoria of the discovery of a new Ogoni Moses, the people believed that there was no obstacle to their freedom that they could not scale. These empowered people from 1992 adopted a "global" handle to their struggle.

It is interesting to note that MOSOP's initial attempts at globalising Ogoni resistance met with failure. Saro-Wiwa, MOSOP's spokesman, recalled his disappointment in 1991:

> I telephoned Greenpeace. 'We don't work in Africa', was the chilling reply I got. And when I called up Amnesty, I was asked, 'Is anyone dead?' 'Is anyone in gaol?' And when I replied in the negative, I was told nothing could be done.

Yet, Saro-Wiwa and MOSOP were not put off, and the following year, 1992, the movement connected the Unrepresented Nations and Peoples Organisation (UNPO), based in The Hague, in The Netherlands, part-home of Shell and established some networks and contacts within the international NGO community. MOSOP used an important global event the United Nations declaration of 1993 as the Year of Indigenous Peoples, to launch the Ogoni struggle through a huge rally of over 300,000 Ogoni people on January 4, 1993. This action demonstrated MOSOP's popularity in Ogoniland, and showed the people that the world knew of their plight, and recognised the justness of their cause. For the ordinary Ogoni, the wide media coverage that the event received was concrete proof that they had captured national and international attention. This recognition boosted their dignity, and their sense of national pride and solidarity. Since 1993, January 4 has been celebrated every year as Ogoni day in spite of the heavy military presence. This way a global event has become a local idiom of Ogoni solidarity and "nationalism".

Another element that turned out to be alarming to the Nigerian state was the way it was totally bypassed by MOSOP in connecting to the global arena. The image of MOSOP "escaping" from the clutches of the Nigerian state opened up the authorities at Abuja to accusations of inefficiency by the oil multinationals, and made the state more desperate to demonstrate its relevance both as the legitimate authority and mediator (gatekeeper) between the world and the Ogoni. The way this was demonstrated through violent and cruel means only worsened matters and provided more evidence with which MOSOP empowered its appeals to the "global".

The UNPO experience, and other trips to Europe and the United states also strengthened MOSOP's capacity on the strategies of waging an international campaign, which global forum or platform to use, and what medium of publicity to adopt in globalising the Ogoni struggle. That same year, MOSOP's case was for the first time placed before a global assembly—the United Nations Working Group on Indigenous Populations. Saro-Wiwa's presentation painted a picture of the Ogoni people as an indigenous people, discriminated against, expropriated, and facing imminent genocide, from the wanton destruction of the environmental basis of their existence by the activities of the oil industry, and the extractive and repressive activities of the militarised Nigerian state (Saro-Wiwa, 1995):

> Petroleum was discovered in Ogoni in 1958 and since then an estimated US hundred billion dollars' worth of oil and gas has been carted away from Ogoni land. In return for this, the Ogoni people have received nothing. Oil exploration has turned Ogoni into a waste land: lands, streams, and creeks are totally and continually polluted; the atmosphere has been poisoned, charged as it is with hydro-carbon vapours, methane, carbon monoxide, carbon dioxide and soot emitted by gas which has been flared twenty-four hours a day for thirty-three years in very close proximity to human habitation.

On a very interesting note Ken linked the intensified exploitation of Ogoni oil to the IMF/World Bank programme of structural adjustment:

> Nigeria has an external debt of over thirty billion dollars. None of that debt was incurred on any project in the Ogoni area or on any project remotely beneficial

to the Ogoni. The International Monetary Fund and the World Bank, keen on the payment of the debt, are encouraging intensified exploitation of oil and gas, which constitute 94 per cent of Nigeria's Gross Domestic Product. Such exploitation is against the wishes of the Ogoni people as it only worsens the degradation of the Ogoni environment and the decimation of the Ogoni people.

Another aspect of the globalisation of the Ogoni struggle was through the documentary films which showed the savage destruction of the Ogoni environment by Shell, and the ruthless repression of the Ogoni by the Nigerian military to shocked audiences in the UK, Europe and other parts of the world. The earliest of such films was "The Heat of the Moment", followed by others, such as "Drilling Fields", and "Delta Force". MOSOP organised lecture tours, seminars and campaigns through which the Ogoni message was further pressed home. In no time, the global NGO and rights community, including Greenpeace and Amnesty International had adopted the MOSOP campaign. Ken Saro-Wiwa was given several awards in Europe and North America (two examples of such, were the Right Livelihood Award and the Goldman Environmental Prize) in recognition of his contributions to the environmental and human rights struggle of the Ogoni. Some of the groups that backed MOSOP's claims globally included: Human Rights Watch Africa, FIAN International, Article 19, Inter Rights, the Body Shop, Friends of the Earth, Sierra Club, Rain Forest Action Network, Project Underground, Delta, Trocaire, World Council of Churches, Book Aid International, and the Netherlands Committee of the International Union for the Conservation of Nature. They provided support, physically visited the delta to investigate MOSOP's claims and accusations against Shell and the state. Their findings, documenting the repression of the Ogoni, and the involvement of Shell and the military, were compiled, published and given publicity world-wide (Boele, 1995; Crow, 1995; Robinson, 1996; Human Rights Watch, 1999). This as it were, completed the connecting of the local cause to the global movement, globalising the Ogoni cause, and localising global struggles in Ogoni.

There is no doubt that the packaging of the Ogoni as a tiny people faced with the combined might of Shell and the Nigerian state, empowered MOSOP's appeals and complaints to the international community. The adoption of the Ogoni case internationally meant that the international rights, and NGO, community used the global platform to expose the environmental damage and violation of rights in Ogoni land being perpetrated by Shell and the Nigerian state. Exposés on Shell's excesses in the delta hurt the company's image in Europe and North America, and also showed its double standards regarding corporate responsibility and maintenance of environmental standards. For while Shell played by the rules on its home-grounds in Europe and North America, the same standard was seen as being out of place in its oil colonies such as Ogoni. Thus, the global adoption of the Ogoni campaign hit Shell hard.

The Ogoni case also received wide coverage in the local and international news media. Leading international newspapers and news magazines reported the events in Ogoni and wrote editorials on the violation of human and environmental rights in the Niger delta. Catma Films also did a couple of documentaries (The Heat of the Moment and Delta Force) which captured and conveyed living pictures of the ecological terror and the suffering of the Ogoni under military repression to a shocked western audience on Channel 4 (Catma, 1992, 1995). A particularly damaging instance was when an ex-Shell official (head of environmental studies), Bop Van Dessel in a documentary shown on Granada television confessed that Shell was polluting the Niger delta (Clotheir and O'Conner, 1996). The globalisation of the Ogoni struggle peaked after the November 1995 hanging of the "Ogoni nine", and the international outcry that followed. More groups and even some governments and international organisations joined in sharply criticising Shell and the Nigerian state for their actions. Nigeria instantly became a pariah nation, while most EU and western countries temporarily re-called their ambassadors based in Nigeria.

Many MOSOP radicals, NYCOP and FOWA cadres went underground or escaped into exile. Offices of Ogoni resistance sprang up in the UK, the USA and Canada. Ledum Mitee took over as Acting President of MOSOP, and coordinated the struggle against Shell and the state from Europe. MOSOP continued to issue press releases on developments in the Niger delta, organised the celebration of Ogoni Day in spite of the heavy military presence in Ogoni land, and insisted on the demands contained in the OBR. An international campaign was organised for the release of the 20 youths in detention pending trial for the murder of the 4 Ogoni elders, alongside the insistence that Shell would not re-enter Ogoni, if it continued to refuse to enter into dialogue with MOSOP. From a position of relative obscurity, ethnic identity politics in the Niger delta was not just on the front-burner of the national question, it had become a matter of grave concern and a lot of activity at the global level.

After MOSOP's successful use of the global platform to project its complaints and appeals, inviting in the process a state and global backlash, its example did not go unnoticed in other parts of the delta. In spite of the "displacement" of the Ogoni case from the forefront of the global agenda by other global hotspots such as the crisis in the Great Lakes region and the Kosovo conflict, other groups in the delta are still "connecting" to the global level. An equally sophisticated struggle is now being waged alongside MOSOP's own, by the Ijaw Youth Congress, which is also adopting the global rights discourse and platform to empower its claims and appeals. Their struggles are being broadly supported by the same western rights NGOs even though a few may have "dropped off", either as a result of the "Green Backlash" (Rowell, 1996) or a split, or a movement to newer, more "exciting" global "hotspots".

The approach is wider in the sense that the case is made on behalf of the Niger delta, and there is a larger measure of networking among groups in the Niger delta connecting the local to the global. An activist like Oronto Douglas (IYC/ERA) has toured Europe and the United States presenting the case of the Niger delta to the world. Information on MOSOP and IYC, and other oil minorities struggles can be found on the Internet, where many international rights groups have continued to give support and show solidarity with the people of the Niger delta. The excesses of oil multinationals are daily investigated and reported to the world by the popular oil minorities movements in the Niger delta, particularly the IYC and Chikoko, and rights groups such as the ERA, and the ND-HERO. Indeed, hundreds of groups and individuals world-wide have criticised the recent violent backlash against protesting Ijaw youth, expressed solidarity with the IYC, and criticised oil multinationals for operating in such a conflict-ridden region (The Guardian, 1999b).

The resurgence of ethnic identity politics through the oil minorities movement of the Niger delta has given a new complexion to the intersection between environmental conflict and the struggle for self-determination in a still emerging post-cold war order. What is interesting is the trend in the Niger delta where the deeper entrenchment of globalised oil relations is dialectically feeding an equally globalised movement of resistance with very strong popular local roots. A formidable challenge, therefore, lies ahead for global oil capital, if it does not change from its conquistadorial ways which may turn out to be its Waterloo in the twenty-first century.

Decay and Renewal in the Oil Minorities Movements of the Niger Delta

The oil minorities movements, which act as the major bearers of ethnic identity politics in the Niger delta today, are still undergoing transformations that reflect processes of decay and renewal. These movements are neither homogenous, nor have they reached the final stages of becoming "movements for themselves". They continue to harbour contradictory tendencies and factions, which struggle even within themselves to determine the broad direction, and contents of the demands of the movement. Such contradictory tendencies and factions include: elders versus the youth, democracy versus dictatorship, conservatives versus radicals, collaborators versus militants, jingoists versus pan-delta nationalists, people versus the oil multinationals, people versus the state, even capitalists versus leftists. These divisions or contradictions are themselves fluid, and do not preclude alliances across the trenches when issues bordering on survival and the broad Niger delta agenda are concerned: increased share and control of oil revenues, repeal of exploitative laws, bigger compensation for oil pollution, development of the Niger delta, employment and provision of good social welfare.

The flash-points of conflict operate at various levels: struggles over scarce resources, personality differences, communal rivalry, intra-elite struggles for power, positions in globalised oil relations, inter-generational (youth versus elders) "wars" and the very nature of the democratic content of the agenda of self-determination in the Niger delta. It is these contradictions spawned by the dialectics of state and globalised oil capital that drive the transformations of the oil minorities movement in the Niger delta.

Even the Nigerian state in carrying out its role of mediating globalised oil relations, has its own contradictions which reflect its subordination to global oil capital, while itself being a site for struggles by a hegemonic elite intent on maximising the gains of the primitive accumulation of oil wealth. This means that the state in its mediatory politics reflects both tendencies vis à vis its dealings with the oil minorities: military repression side by side with the co-optation of willing oil minorities' elite. This ambivalence has worsened the tension in the delta, and deepened the cleavages in the minorities movement especially those who are willing to co-operate with the state, and those who refuse to, and push for its restructuring in line with aspirations of popular sovereignty and local autonomy for the delta.

The point is that the ambivalence of the Nigerian state especially under adjustment dialectically has fed into the popularisation of the oil minorities movement. Social crises in the delta have meant that the legitimacy of the federal government continues to wear thin in the Niger delta. This process has enhanced the renewal of these movements in opposition to the extractive power of state and oil, widened their social base, and opened up space at the top for an alternative leadership untainted by the "gatekeeper and benefit-capture syndrome", to emerge.

Another phenomenon that characterised the transformation process was the upsurge in violent inter-communal conflicts. These were either violent conflicts over shrinking resources (land and water), communal boundaries, and the explosion of latent rivalries and feuds often instigated by the oil multinationals and/or the state. The latter trend was often in a bid to create confusion and a pretext under which the government could intervene to restore order. While the confusion was often a ploy, though not entirely successful, to divert attention from any concerted effort by the communities to form a united pan-delta front against the state and the oil multinationals, it has in some cases led to reverses in some of the oil minorities movements. A number of examples will suffice: the case of the Ogoni versus their neighbours (Andoni, Okrika and Ndoki) in 1993–94 (Robinson, 1996:59–61), the Okpoma versus Brass clashes in January 1999 (ND-HERO, 1999). Perhaps the worst case of inter-communal, inter-ethnic stife, is the bloody conflicts between the Ijaw and their neighbours (Itsekiri, Edo, Ilaje and parts of Urhobo), that have resulted in the killing of thousands of people on all sides, and which still erupts into episodic outbursts of violence. Of all the conflicts between the Ijaw and their neighbours, that involving the Itsekiri since 1997 has been the most violent and prolonged (Efenakpo and Okanlawon, 1997; Ofuokwu, 1998; INC-USA, 1999b). The immediate trigger was the alleged transfer of the capital of the newly created Warri South West Local Government from Ogbe Ijaw an Ijaw settlement to Ogidigben, an Itsekiri settlement. In spite of efforts by the government and other interested parties to resolve the crisis, peace has not returned as both sides have continued to launch surprise attacks on each other's settlements in the maze of creeks, swamps and islands in the Niger delta.

The Ijaw are being accused by their neighbours of nursing an expansionist agenda in the delta, and exploiting their connections to the military to achieve their plan for a "greater" Ijaw nation. In response, the Ijaws have denied nursing such ambitions, pointing accusing fingers at the oil multinationals and the Nigerian state as those provoking the conflict between the Ijaw and their neighbours, who had lived in relative peace over the decades. The curious issue is the blame placed on the military by both sides, either for fomenting conflict, or looking the other way while one ethnic group is bludgeoning the other (IEF, 1999a, IEF, 1999b; INC-USA, n.d; INC-USA, 1999b; Vanguard, 1999; Communiqué of Itsekiri Patriots, 1999). The result is a lot of needless bloodletting, waste and distrust among the various ethnic minorities in the delta.

In all these conflicts, guerrilla-like tactics and sophisticated weapons have been used. Many people have been displaced, living as refugees in towns and cities far from their homes, and never knowing exactly if they would ever return to their villages to pick up the pieces of their lives. As in the Ogoni case, there are strong allegations of Nigerian military covert involvement in the outbreak of communal violence in the delta. This takes various forms: through the infiltration of certain communities by soldiers on a mission to destabilise another one that has been causing "trouble" for government as in the case of the Ogoni versus their neighbours. It could involve the training and arming of communal youth armies by retired military personnel and other local notables intent on righting certain historical wrongs visited on their people, or through military "physical force" proponents who are keen on demonstrating the practical advantages of the coercive pacification of the delta. The problem with this approach is that increasingly the options for trust, constructive dialogue and political give-and-take are being narrowed, while that of settling conflict through force and violence seems to be gaining ground.

A lot has been said already about the inter-generational war in the delta, and the ways in which it is upturning and re-creating certain traditional norms of power and authority. This in itself feeds into tensions within the movements as the radicals and youth re-define ethnic identity socially. The elders have been placed in a dilemma: either to adopt the popular agenda, retain their legitimacy, but at the risk of incurring the wrath of the state-MNOC alliance, or to assert their traditional authority in curbing the rising influence of the radicals and youth. Across the delta, the youth are defying the traditional elders and conservatives who still subscribe to the state-MNOC agenda, except in cases where the elders have been able to demonstrate their credibility and commitment to the people. Yet, this has implications for the leadership of the oil minorities movement, and cohesion within the oil producing communities. Beyond this, it will define the way the national question will be handled in Nigeria. For the state of flux in the oil minorities which is currently showing an ascendancy of popular forces is bound to push for a nation-state project based on social justice, local autonomy, and the decentralisation of power and resource control.

Closely related to the generation issue, is that of the re-definition of traditional authority and the place of traditional rulers/elders. As a part of the "delta ruling class", the traditional rulers/elders had a "dual identity", as partners of the federal establishment and the oil multinationals, and as the custodians of cultural and traditional authority. Usually, the "bigger" traditional rulers and influential elders got more largesse and wielded more influence, over larger communities or constituencies. They were useful instruments of social control in the neglected and impoverished oil communities, until the economic crisis and state authoritarianism began to erode their legitimacy. Thus, when oil minorities movements re-emerged in the late 1980s, traditional movements played a part both as legitimisers of ethnic identity, and instruments of social control.

In the case of Umuechem, as well as other oil communities, several traditional rulers have been caught in the "cross fire" between the forces of repression and resistance. Others have been killed by security forces (Umuechem), others have been "exiled" by their own people, and most are caught somewhere in between (Ollor-Obari, 1999d:40; INC, 1999). These have in the main trod the delicate path of serving as "honest brokers" between the angry youth and the federal authorities, urging restraint on both sides, calling for dialogue, and the withdrawal of troops from the delta (Ollor-Obari, 1999e:56; Okafor, 1999:48). Even among the honest brokers, most of them are under a lot of pressure from the youth to adopt and confer legitimacy on the popular agenda. Thus, like the local ruling elite, the traditional class is fragmented. To give a recent example, while a faction of Ijaw elders in the INC made a joint statement supporting the Kaiama Declaration, another faction of Ijaw elders in the INC supported by some traditional rulers responded with a condemnation of the same declaration (Ollor-Obari, 1998e:7; The Guardian, 1998:3). Similar schisms within Ogoni elders, and between them and the youth contributed to the crisis within MOSOP, which led to the murder of the four chiefs and the repression that followed, forcing the Ogoni "revolution" into retreat. The wounds inflicted on the Ogoni are just beginning to heal in a painfully slow manner. The divisions within the oil minorities notwithstanding, it is still possible to see that the ethnic minority nationality movements are still being transformed from a grassroots/popular perspective.

What flows from the foregoing is that ethnic identity politics in the Niger delta by the oil minorities movements is being socially redefined to reflect the power and influence of the popular classes in the delta. This "revolution from below", is however being challenged vigorously by forces both within and outside the Niger delta. At the heart of the processes of renewal and decay taking place in the oil minorities movements in the delta, are these contradictions which are daily being reproduced and resolved in the course of the struggles of the people for local autonomy, resource (land) control and their human and environmental rights as citizens of Nigeria. What trajectories these movements will follow, hold significant implications for the future of the nation-state project in Nigeria.

Trajectories of Ethnic Minority Politics in the Niger Delta: Implications for the Nation-State Project in Nigeria

From the foregoing, there is no gainsaying that the volatile trajectories of ethnic minority politics hold certain implications for the future of democracy, and the nation-state project in Nigeria. There has been for some time now a debate over what the struggles mean for the Nigerian state. Among the military strategists and proponents of the statist approach to security, the rumblings in the Niger delta are a potent threat to national stability and must be dealt with by physical force. This position is informed by several considerations: over 70 per cent of Nigeria's petroleum and gas is produced in the region, accounting for the bulk of Nigeria's wealth, the region hosts investments in the Nigerian oil industry worth hundreds of billions of dollars making it the heart of Nigeria's monocultural economy. Others include historical and political factors: the suspicion that certain interests can seize upon the long history of oil minority struggles for self-determination to subvert the country, concerns that the voicing of grievances can spread to other aggrieved communities outside the delta. There is also the suspicion that if not contained, the protests can grow into separatist agitation, secession and the possible disintegration of Nigeria. At the core of all this is the determination to ensure that Nigeria remains safe for oil-based accumulation and the global market. This is borne out by the fact that without oil-based accumulation, the ruling class that has "privatised" the Nigerian state will lose out on the providential wealth that only oil bestows on those who control it, to the exclusion of others. The intersection of the narrow interests of this class and those of global oil, defines their control of oil by their control of Nigeria.

On the other hand, are those who assert that the issues being raised by the oil minorities are fundamental to the resolution of the national question, and the adjustments or modifications in political structures and processes which can advance such a resolution. Their position is hinged on the following consideration: that the demands of the oil minorities interrogate the inequitable and undemocratic character of the Nigerian state. It exemplifies the historical struggles for liberation from exploitation, oppression and domination to which all people aspire. Furthermore, the struggles also provide a nationalist platform against foreign domination and exploitation, and reinforce the view that national security cannot be separated from the welfare and equality of every Nigerian citizen irrespective of ethnic affiliation, state of origin or class.

There is, therefore, a division between those who fear that attending to the demands of the oil minorities may provoke the disintegration of the nation-state, and endanger their monopoly of power and oil; and others who are keen on transforming the status quo to ensure the equality of access to power and the democratic control of power. This latter position is informed by the knowledge that the oil minorities' question cannot be resolved independent or outside of the democratic resolution of the national question. The issue is broadly posed as decentralising the monopolistic highly-centralised command structure of governance that has undermined the spirit of federalism, and bred all forms of inequities, inequalities and disparities within the Nigerian nation-state. These debates have grown alongside the shrinking legitimacy of the Nigerian state, and received more potency following the post-June 12, 1993 national crisis, and have provided aggrieved groups with the space to state their case, and push a social-national agenda. Thus, in spite of the contradictions besetting the oil minorities movement, they have been able to place their demands at the centre of the debates over Nigeria's political future.

Before going further, it is apposite to re-visit the core concerns in the debates over the national question in Nigeria, and the clash between a homogenising, western-style nation-state project, and one that advocates a national unity project that upholds the rich multiplicity of plural identities based on dialogue, equity, popular sovereignty, local autonomy, and equal access to power and resources. (Olukoshi and Agbu, 1996; Soyinka, 1996), strike at the heart of the debate, especially the twin issues of political power and revenue allocation (Mustapha, 1986):

> These debates were not so much concerned with the creation of more states and local governments as with a significant reduction in the powers of the federal government in order to allow for a greater equality of access to power and resources by federating units that enjoy substantive autonomy (Olukoshi and Agbu, 1996:75).

It is therefore not difficult to see how the trajectories of the oil minorities movement of the Niger delta "log into" this national debate, and how the debate legitimises and reproduces the demands of the oil minorities. An examination of the Ogoni Bill of Rights, Addendum to the Ogoni Bill of Rights, and the Kaiama Declaration (see Appendices), shows they all place emphasis on autonomy, control of oil and land. They also seek equal access and representation in national institutions, compensation and restitution from the oil companies for environmental degradation and violation of rights. These demands impinge on the central issues of the national debate and the need for a social consensus. The demands of these minority movements also validate the observation that the traditional approaches to federal governance in Nigeria: states creation, revenue allocation, local governments creation, application of federal character, and the establishment of institutions to manage the devolution of powers have not solved the problems caused by the post-civil war centralisation of political and economic power in Nigeria. Clearly the issue of the day is no longer the cynical comment that the oil minorities are not the only aggrieved ethnic nationality in Nigeria, but how to negotiate a national resolution, recognising their peculiar position and needs, and addressing such along with other issues in the national question. The resolution of the oil minorities' question is important because of their strategic position in Nigeria's political economy, and the imperatives of social justice, national reconciliation and forgiveness which should form the foundation of sustainable democracy in the next republic.

What the above shows is that the oil minorities' question is inextricably linked to the democratic question in Nigeria. The urgency with which this needs to be re-addressed is perhaps best underscored with the deepening of national socio-economic crisis, and the rate at which the legitimacy of the Nigerian state is fast being eroded across the Niger delta. A few examples will suffice. In 1993, the Ogoni boycotted the June 12, 1993 elections, largely on the grounds that they did not want to confer legitimacy on an election conducted under an undemocratic 1989 federal constitution. Electoral officers were stopped from distributing voting materials, and some were assaulted, and election material hijacked. Elections did not take place in Ogoniland (Lukula, 1993:6). The same scenario broadly replayed itself in 1999, when the Ijaw in Bayelsa state mostly boycotted the February 1999 elections. Armed youth and protesters have confronted federal troops, kidnapped expatriate oil company staff, and blocked flow stations, oil platforms, in defiance of the militarisation of the delta by the federal state. Recently, the announcement of a N15.3 billion development plan for the Niger delta by the federal government has been criticised for being "vulnerable to diversion" and not involving the people in decision-making at all stages of development design, planning and implementation (The Guardian, April, 27, 1999). Indeed the level of doubt that such a programme will succeed where earlier efforts have failed is high. As Ibiba Don-Pedro reports (The Guardian, April 28, 1999a):

> There are fears that Abubakar's panel would end up as ineffectual bodies such as OMPADEC set up in 1992 by the Gen. Ibrahim Babangida administration, the Directorate of Foods, Roads and Rural Infrastructure (DFRI) headed by AVM Larry Koinyan (rtd) which only served to produce millionaires of a few contractors and members of the traditional ruling class in the oil producing areas.

The meetings with the oil minorities involving the out-going head of state, General Abubakar, and the incoming "civilian" head of state, General Obasanjo, who even tried to mediate between the FMG and the Ijaw youth have not had much impact on the crisis. General Obasanjo's intervention did not cut much ice with the delta youth that hold him responsible for the 1978 Land Use Act, which dispossessed the oil minorities of their land (Osunde, 1999a; Olufemi and Don-Pedro, 1999). Also, they are of the opinion that the current transition (which produced Obasanjo as President) is undemocratic, hence they want no part of it, insisting instead on a sovereign national conference involving all ethnic nationalities in Nigeria (Adeoye, 1999; Olufemi and Ollor-Obari, 1999). The ability of these movements to bypass the state and directly connect to the global arena, their access to arms, and the exposure of mass theft of billions of Naira by some key actors in the Abacha regime have further worsened the crisis of state legitimacy, empowered their demands and the margin of terror in the Niger delta.

In spite of the increased frequency and intensity of intra- and intercommunal clashes, and the violence involved, in the quest for access to resources (land, oil, compensation), and power, there is no doubt, that ethnic identity politics in the delta has become a potent challenge to the present structure of the Nigerian nation-state. State structures have been unable to mediate the revolutionary pressures from below, and in the process, have largely become parts of the problem of the "irrelevance" of the extractive state. No doubt, the military approach of "physical force", and the distribution of largesse to the largely discredited colluding elite/elders in the delta have not helped matters. It has raised the stakes, embraced violence and rejected dialogue, and bred feelings of alienation, anger, distrust and victimisation among the aggrieved oil minorities of the Niger delta.

Concluding Remarks: Niger Delta Oil Minorities Movement and the Future of Nigeria

The fate of the oil minorities of the Niger delta and that of Nigeria are inextricably linked together. Nigeria needs the oil and gas in the delta, she has virtually limitless human and natural resources there, while the delta needs Nigeria to mediate its multiple pluralities and contradictions and continue along the path of a historically grounded politico-cultural union founded on the post-colonial, post-oil boom national project. It also needs Nigeria for security and strategic reasons, not unrelated to the volatility of global oil politics, and the nature of oil as a wasting asset. Yet, the lesson that comes out forcefully from the analysis so far, is that though both Nigeria and the oil minorities have been together, the basis of that "belongingness" is being interrogated, and stands the risk of being rejected if a re-negotiation fails to take place, or fails after taking place. As Olukoshi and Agbu (1996:96) caution:

> For although unity may be desirable, it can neither be taken for granted or assumed away nor can it be treated as something static or too sacrosanct to be openly negotiated. While the use of force and state terror may create a semblance of unity, it can never provide an enduring basis for it. In essence, if unity is to be sustainable, it has to be based on consent, rooted in the existence of a legitimate state and government to which people freely give their allegiance in return for certain basic socio-economic and political rights.

The starting point for an oil minorities-Nigerian nation-state nexus is the establishment of a democratic order in Nigeria that can create an atmosphere conducive for a political process of give and take to thrive. Nowhere in their demands have the oil minorities movements asked to secede from the Nigerian federation, implying that they seek nothing beyond political restructuring to give greater autonomy to the federating units and ethnic nationalities, and guarantee equal access to power and resources. Yet, it is the nature of these demands that strikes at the heart of the centralisation of economic and political power upon which the post-civil war ruling class is built. For this hegemonic class that is in crisis itself, the demands for change are calculated to exploit its vulnerabilities, hence its resistance to change, lest it loses out completely in its hold on power.

At the current conjuncture of a deepening economic crisis, multiple crises at the level of state legitimacy and governance manifested as a deep-seated national crisis, there is really no other option to re-designing the Nigerian federation. And it can only be done in a democratic context where the people are free to organise and express themselves politically, and where social questions (injustice, inequity, identity etc.) can be engaged in a constructive manner. The idea of an elected national assembly need not be incompatible with the notion of a sovereign national conference. The national assembly can either embark on immediate entrenchment of fresh clauses in the 1999 Federal constitution that would guarantee democratic constitutionalism, or facilitate a national conference with representations from all interest groups, and ethnic nationalities in Nigeria. Either of both options if honestly and purposefully pursued would form an egalitarian cauldron for national unity. But it must be emphasised that viability and sustainability would depend on "the democratic content of constitution-making and constitutional practice" and the rooting of democracy in popular sovereignty (Olukoshi, 1999:456–458). This would of necessity be based on hard-nosed bargaining between the various interest groups and ethnic nationalities, with a view to arriving at a consensus or a social contract on which basis the national question can be resolved. One agrees with Olukoshi and Agbu (1996:97), when they argue, that; "unity endures where diverse groups feel themselves to be part and parcel of an existing national bargain, do not feel discriminated against in the existing socio-economic and political order, and can tap credible, representative, and responsive channels for the resolution of their grievances". These conditions can only prevail, in a democratic set-up with a popular democratic culture and the rule of law. This brings one back to the original position, that the starting point for the resolution of the national crisis is the establishment of a democratic foundation for Nigerian federalism, and a thriving spirit of "belongingness", based on equal access to all groups on a basis clearly arrived at through bargaining and agreement.

A rather sensitive issue, which is never far beneath the surface in any serious discussion of Nigeria's political future, is the subject of the Nigerian military. While some people are of the opinion that the wise thing to do is to reach a kind of modus vivendi between the civilian and military factions of the Nigerian ruling class, others have rejected such an option outright, blaming the military for being the greatest obstacle to democracy in Nigeria. In between the middle of the road school has blamed the politicised officers and the opportunistic elite for the travails of democracy in Nigeria. The first option has failed largely because of the poor record of the military in governance particularly since 1985 and the inability of the ruling class to amicably settle the matter of who should head the military-civilian arrangement and the terms and name for such a political invention. This has also been worsened by the internal contradictions within the class, greed, the personalisation of power by individuals (so-called strongmen), and the betrayal of public trust and confidence by crass opportunism, thievery, and a shocking lack of foresight and vision by the ruling elite. A lot of Nigerians have grown openly cynical of the possibility of this class ever being capable of midwifing democracy, and playing according to the rules. It is further complicated by the fact that the military class, which controls immense resources and wields substantial influence, still seeks to control power even after leaving office. Furthermore, it feels like a fish out of water once out of government, and lives in mortal dread that a real transfer of power to the people could lead to the military class being called to account for their past misdeeds, public humiliation and the confiscation of their loot.

In order to bridge the factional divide between the military and civilian factions of the ruling class, there has been a civilianisation of the "politicised military" via the entry of retired top military officers into political parties and the traditional feudal ruling class (as traditional rulers, chiefs etc.). But this is clearly not going to solve the problem; indeed, it would spark off a new struggle between ex-military generals and their civilian political counterparts for power and authority in the political system. In what is usually regarded as the natural preserve of the civilians—democratic politics—some have called for a return to a military professionalism that recognises the subordination of the military to civilian authorities as the perfect solution to the menace of coupism. This expectation is both a historical considering the origins of the military as a weapon of the colonial state and the emergence of a hegemonic bloc within the military establishment exploiting its hold over the state and its ties with international capital (especially oil capital) to transform itself into a ruling class. For somewhere in between, the line separating the professional from the political became blurred, and is continuously reproduced, expanded and strengthened by present and future military political office-holders, and coup plotters. The military is thus reflective of the contradictions and struggles in everyday Nigerian life: class, ethnic nationality, religion, factional, personal etc. In its unsuccessful bid to mediate the larger contradictions in politics and society, the Nigerian military has become a part of the national crisis.

What the foregoing shows is that the de-politicisation of the military, and its subordination to democratic governance is a complex, difficult but necessary part of the democratisation of the Nigerian state. Several options present themselves. The military should submit itself to the national process of healing and reconciliation, and re-define its professionalisation in a democratic ambience. But the most feasible option is that Nigerians themselves should ultimately determine what kind of national military they want. This still brings us back to the imperative of a national bargain, that will among many other things, work out the ways the military can be weaned of its political adventurism which is largely obstructive of social justice, democracy, and development.

Still on the national level, is the challenge of national economic recovery and development. There is no doubt that the current national crisis is both a manifestation of gross economic mismanagement and a symptom of economic crisis. Without going into much detail, the present economic crisis is in reality the crisis of oil-based accumulation in Nigeria. Therefore its roots and ultimate solution lie in the "political" and the ways distortions in the oil economy are eliminated or managed. The people must politically control the economy, define its priorities, direction and targets, and deal with problems such as corruption, waste, accountability, injustices and uneven development. The reality of a globalised world implies that a balance will need to be struck between the demands of economic rationality and those of social welfare, and the need to institutionalise accountability, transparency, merit, public service and democratic governance. Thus, external conditionalities that seek to impose inappropriate policies in the name of "adjustment" or "economic reform" and detached or distorted assumptions would have no place, and would be rejected in such a democratic context.

The national context of the resolution of the national question, though the most important, cannot be totally abstracted from or separated from the global. In an era of rapid globalisation, programmes like structural adjustment, the free reign given to market forces to over-run primary product exporters, or monocultural economies, the inequitable structure of international trade and the activities of powerful multinationals continue to complicate the economic and political crisis confronting African states. There has to be a reopening of the debate on the nature of, and implications of vertical North-South economic relations, with a view to pushing the nuclei of globalisation to respect the right of nation-states in the South to attend to the welfare and developmental needs of the majority of their own people, which may not necessarily fall under the rubric of "profit". The ways foreign capital has operated in national contexts have serious implications for the democratic project (and the nation-state). Obviously hiding behind the cloak of non-interference global big business, for example the oil multinationals in Nigeria have made huge profits in contexts characterised by the lack of development, accountability, transparency, and the wanton violation of human rights. In the case of Shell Petroleum Development Corporation for instance, it has been shown that political instability in Nigeria has not adversely affected the steady expansion of its investments or the huge profits it is making out of the Nigerian oil industry (Frynas, 1998:457-78). It is thus hardly surprising therefore that in spite of all the hue and cry over community unrest in the delta, and non-payment of the state's share of joint-venture cash calls, Shell in February 1999, announced plans to make an $8.5 billion investment in the Nigerian oil industry and raise the country's oil and gas reserves (EIU, 1999:30).

There is an urgent need for a revision of corporate governance to reflect not just the concern for profit, but the welfare of the people and the development of the host-nation-state. Already there are signs of a gradual paradigm-shift in terms of community relations from the top-down tokenism, laden with PR considerations to one of community participatory development. However this approach is yet to be fully translated into policy, and is still shrouded in public relations considerations while providing work for expatriate "consultants". It would seem that it is a ploy by oil multinationals (working through NGOs and local CBOs) to appropriate the discourse of developmental INGOs to prettify the face of oil companies operating in oil communities. This "shift" is more of form than content. What must be done is to push the shift more towards the direction of democratising community development at all stages of the policy process, and making the people of the oil producing communities the centrepiece of such policies.

The external context can strengthen the restructuring of the nation-state project in Nigeria if its strengthens local capacities, and provides an international arena that is fairer to the country's aspirations. The discourse on human and environmental rights needs to be matched with action at the international level. Companies that operate under the shield of repressive states and gatekeepers must be liable to sanctions. In the same way companies that fail to operate at internationally recognised standards of environmental safety should be made accountable to an international tribunal to which aggrieved people can appeal. A post-cold war order founded on global inequity and double standards may turn out to be more conflict-laden and unfair than the one it replaced. The deepening of market relations across the globe, and the fetish being made of economic rationality and market reforms particularly as they relate to Africa need to be re-visited as a way of mitigating some of the external sources of crisis on the continent. That way, the contradictions that globalisation creates and reproduces can be better mediated as part of the resolution of the national crisis.

It will not suffice to focus on the national and global, without zeroing in on the micro or local level—the Niger delta. Issues of control of land and the re-distribution of resources to redress current inequities are fundamental and urgent. Even though the case of the oil minorities has been well articulated, and there is no doubt that they have had a bad deal within the post-civil war federal project, there is a need for them to begin to address some of their own internal contradictions. First of all there is the need of the oil minorities to transcend the current divisions in their ranks, and adopt non-violent modalities of conflict resolution whether they are dealing with communal, regional or national conflicts. Secondly in putting all their eggs in the "oil basket", the people face the risk of neglecting even that which they can do for themselves relying on community-based approaches to natural resources management and community development. Admittedly, this may be difficult considering what the people have suffered, the pervasive influence of being socialised into an "oil culture", and the pent up rage and frustrations that have welled up over time. Yet, laying themselves open for manipulation by various internal and external forces seeking to prey upon their anger, rivalries, hunger, and feuds, may not in the end work in favour of the oil minorities. An agenda of internal unity and cohesion must objectively become part of the liberation agenda of the oil minorities, which will in turn feed a popular-democratic project.

An important step towards guaranteeing a stable and sustainable future for a democratic Nigeria, includes the making of restitution to the oil minorities of the Niger delta. The federal government needs to devolve powers in a way that promotes popular participation in the decision-making process, and guarantees a measure of local autonomy to all the federating units, including those in the Niger delta. While the approach to the allocation of oil revenue has been incremental and federally driven, the time has come to move in a new direction. The current increment of allocative principle of oil derivation from 3 to 13 per cent may not be the real issue after all. Whatever percentage is adopted should be arrived at only after a careful consideration of the developmental needs of the delta along with the credible representatives of the oil minorities. Beyond this, the oil producing communities should control allocated revenues and resources, and it is they that should then be accountable, both to their people and the nation, on how, and on what they expended the resources. The issues of the control of oil and land remain sore points that must be healed. Decrees that alienate the people completely from oil and their land need to be replaced by laws that balance considerations of fairness and social justice with those of equitable and sustainable national development.

Ultimately, the changing forms of identity politics in the Niger delta greatly enrich the debates around the establishment of an enduring and cohesive basis for a democratic federal nation-state, if the Nigerian state is to be guaranteed a meaningful future in the twenty-first century. The way it engages the question of citizenship, identity, oil and class strongly suggests that without dealing with these issues at a national level, the issues of development, democracy and federalism risk becoming a big question mark on Nigeria's future. The final solution is inextricably tied to the possibilities of a developmental and democratic state in Nigeria founded upon popular sovereignty and democratic practices.

References

Abimboye, D. 1990. "Massacre at Dawn", *African Concord*, December 3.
Adebayo, A. 1988. "Revenue Allocation: A Historical Analysis of the Nigerian Experience", in Olaniyan, Richard (ed.), *Federalism in a Changing World*. Lagos: The Presidency.
— 1993. *Embattled Federalism: History of Revenue Allocation in Nigeria, 1936–60*. New York: Peter Lang.
Adebowale, Y. 1998. "Colossal Losses", *Newswatch*, Vol. 28, No. 18.
Adejumobi, S. 1995. "The Structural Adjustment Programme and Multinational Corporations in Nigeria", *Development and Socio-Economic Progress*, Oct–Dec.
Adekanye, S. 1995. "Structural Adjustment, Democratisation and Rising Ethnic Tensions in Africa", *Development and Change*, Vol. 26, No. 2.
Adeoye, A. 1999. "Why Ijaws Oppose Transition" (interview with Oronto Douglas), *Sunday Punch*, February 14.
Adewale, O. 1989. "Oil Spill Compensation Claims in Nigeria, principles, guidelines, criteria", *Journal of African Law*, 33 (1), spring.
— 1990. *Sabotage in the Nigerian Petroleum Industry: Some Socio-Legal Perspectives*. Lagos: Nigerian Institute of Advanced Legal Studies.
Agbu, O. 1998. "Political Opposition and Democratic Transitions in Nigeria, 1985–1996", in Olukoshi, Adebayo (ed.), *The Politics of Opposition in Contemporary Africa*. Uppsala: The Nordic Africa Institute.
Agidee, S. 1999. "Perspective", *Vanguard*, May 17.
Ajayi, A. 1992. "The National Question in Historical Perspective". Text of the Fifth Guardian Newspaper, lecture delivered at the NIIA, Lagos, November 4.
Akande, L. 1999. "Debate in US as Chevron bans radio over Nigeria", *The Guardian*, May 17.
Akanni, T. 1994. "Smoulder on the Water Front", *The Guardian*, January 30.
Ake, C. 1994a. "A People Endangered by Oil", *The Guardian*, August 18.
— 1994b. "War and Terror", *The News*, August 22.
— 1995. "Letter of Resignation from the Steering Committee of the Niger Delta Environmental Survey" (dated November 15, and addressed to Gamaliel Onosode). Reproduced in *The Guardian*, November 24.
— 1996. "Shelling Nigeria Ablaze" (press statement, January 15). Reproduced in *Tell*, January 29.
Akinyele, R. 1990. "States' Creation and Boundary Adjustment in Nigeria 1900–1987: A Study in the Approach to the Problems of Ethnic Minority Groups in Nigeria". Unpublished Ph.D. Dissertation, University of Lagos.
Allagoa, E. and T. Tamuno (eds) 1989. *Land and People of Nigeria: Rivers State*. Port Harcourt: Riverside Communications.
Amnesty International 1993. Extra Judicial Execution/Legal Concern (Nigeria) Agbarator Otu Killed, and 11 Injured, Including Karalolo Korgbara (Female), One Other Detained, May 19.
Amuwo, K. et al. (eds) 1998. *Federalism and Political Restructuring in Nigeria*. Ibadan: Spectrum Books.
Anifowose, R. 1982. *Violence and Politics: The Tiv and Yoruba Experience*. New York: Nok.
Apandem, J. and O. Umanah 1999. "Ijaw Crisis, Seven More Killed: Residents Flee Yenagoa", *The Punch*, January 2.

Apter, A. 1998. "Death and the King's Henchman: Ken Saro-Wiwa and the Political Ecology of Citizenship in Nigeria", in Na' Allah, A. (ed.), *Ogoni's Agonies: Ken Saro-Wiwa and the Crisis in Nigeria*. New Jersey: Africa World Press.

Article 19 1999. Report. "Censorship and Democratic Transition in Nigeria", May 27.

Ashton-Jones, with N. S. Arnott and O. Douglas 1998. *The Human Eco-Systems of the Niger Delta*. Benin City: Environmental Rights Action.

Asiodu, P. 1980. "Impact of Petroleum on the Nigerian Economy", *Public Service Lectures*. Lagos: Federal Civil Service Publications.

Bangura, Y. 1994. *The Search for Identity, Religion and Political Violence*. UNRISD Occasional Paper, No. 6. Geneva: UNRISD.

Bangura, Y. and Peter Gibbon 1992. "Adjustment, Authoritarianism and Democracy in Sub-Saharan Africa: An Introduction to Some Conceptual and Empirical Issues", in Gibbon, Peter, Yusuf Bangura and Arve Ofstad (eds), *Authoritarianism, Democracy and Adjustment: The Politics of Economic Reform in Africa*. Uppsala: The Scandinavian Institute of African Studies.

Barikor-Wiwa, D. 1996. "The Role of Women in the Struggle for Social Justice in Ogoni", *Cultural Review Quarterly*, fall.

Beckman, B. 1981. "Oil, State Expenditure and Class Formation in Nigeria", paper presented to the Conference of the Nordic Association of Political Scientists, Turku, August.

Bello, G. 1998. "Ecological Warfare?", *Tempo*, July 23.

Birnbaum, M. 1995. "Nigeria, Fundamental Rights Denied: Report of the Trial of Ken Saro-Wiwa and Others", Article 19, London.

Boele, R. 1995. "Ogoni: Report of the UNPO Mission to Investigate the Situation of the Ogoni in Nigeria". The Hague: Unrepresented Nations and Peoples Organisation.

Catma Films 1992. "The Heat of the Moment", Channel 4, October 2.

— 1995. "Delta Force", Channel 4, May 4.

Cayford, S. 1996. "The Ogoni Uprising: Human Rights and a Democratic Alternative in Nigeria", *Africa Today*, Vol. 43, No. 2.

Cessou, S. and T. Fatunde 1995. "Nigeria: un regime militaire en sursis", *Jeune Afrique Economie*, July 3.

Chikoko 1997. "In Defence of Our Humanity". Text of address by the Central Committee of the Chikoko Movement at a meeting with journalists in Port Harcourt, September 20.

Civil Liberties Organisation (CLO) 1996. *Ogoni: Trials and Travails*. Lagos: CLO.

Clotheir, P. and E. O'Conner 1996. "Pollution Warnings Ignored by Shell", *The London Guardian*, May, 13.

Communiqué of the Itsekiri Patriots General Conference held in Warri, Delta State of Nigeria on 23–24 January, 1999.

Constitutional Rights Project 1999. "Land, Oil and Human Rights in Nigeria's Delta Region". Lagos: CRP.

Cronje, S. 1972. *The World and Nigeria: The Diplomatic History of the Biafran War 1967–1970*. London: Sidgwick and Jackson.

Crow, M. 1995. "The Ogoni Crisis: A case study of military repression in south-eastern Nigeria", *Human Rights Watch*, Vol. 7, No. 5, July.

Dappa-Biriye, H., R. Briggs, B. Idoniboye-Obu and D. Fubara 1992. "The Endangered Environment of the Niger Delta: Constraints and Strategies". An NGO Memorandum of Rivers' Chiefs and Peoples Conference for the World Conference of Indigenous Peoples on Environment and Development, Rio.

Delta News Release 1999. "Ijaw Youth Council Extend 'Operation Climate Change' Indefinitely, Declare Two Months Period of Mourning for Slain Youths'", January.

Diamond, L., A. Kirk-Greene and Oyeleye Oyediran (eds) 1997. *Transition without End: Nigerian Politics and Civil Society under Babangida*. Ibadan: Vantage Publishers.

Don-Pedro, I. 1999a. "For the Niger Delta, a controversial plan", *The Guardian*, April 28.

— 1999b. "Challenge of the Niger Delta", *The Guardian*, May 24.

Doornbos, M. 1998. "Linking the Future to the Past—Ethnicity and Pluralism", in Mohamed Salih and John Markakis (eds), *Ethnicity and the State in Eastern Africa*. Uppsala: The Nordic Africa Institute.

Douglas, O. 1994. "Ogoni: Four days of brutality and torture", *Liberty*, May–August.

Duodu, C. 1996. "Shell Admits Importing Guns for the Nigerian Police", *The Observer*, January 28.

Economist Intelligence Unit 1998. *Country Report: Nigeria*, Fourth Quarter.

— 1999. *Country Report: Nigeria*, First Quarter.

Efenakpo, and S. Okanlawon 1997. "War of Warri", *The Guardian*, April 26.

Egwu, S. 1998. *Structural Adjustment, Agrarian Change and Rural Ethnicity in Nigeria*. Research report no. 103. Uppsala: The Nordic Africa Institute.

Ekeh, P. and E. Osaghae (eds) 1989. *Federal Character and Federalism in Nigeria*. Ibadan: Heinemann.

Ekpo, A. 1992. "Unemployment and Inflation under Structural Adjustment: The Nigerian Experience", *Eastern Africa Economic Review*, Vol. 8, No. 2.

Environmental Rights Action 1995. *Shell in Iko: The Story of Double Standards*, July 10.

— 1996. *Ogoniland: A Plundered Environment*. Lagos: CLO.

— 1999a. "Carnage at Ekebiri", Field Report No. 22, April 20.

— 1999b. "Ogbogu Raided again for Elf", Field Report No. 23, April 22.

Esajere, A. 1999. "Tough Words for Oil Communities", *The Guardian*, January 1.

Etikerentse, G. 1975. "Some Aspects of the Law Relating to the Oil Industry", paper presented at the National Oil Seminar, September 21–25, published in the Proceedings of the Fourth Annual Oil Seminar GOCON, Lagos.

— 1985. *Nigerian Petroleum Law*. London: Macmillan.

Ezomon, E. 1999a. "In the Delta, the Wounds Run Deep", *The Guardian*, January 29.

— 1999b. "Endless furore over the black gold", *The Guardian*, January 30.

Fact sheet on the Ogoni Struggle, http://www.gem.co.za/ELA/Ogoni.Fact.html

Fadahunsi, A. 1983. *Transnationals and the Oil Industry*. Zaria: CSER, Ahmadu Bello University.

Falola, T. 1988. "The Evolution and Changes in Nigerian Federalism", in Olaniyan, Richard (ed.), *Federalism in a Changing World*. Lagos: The Presidency.

Falola, T. and J. Ihonvbere 1985. *The Rise and Fall of Nigeria's Second Republic, 1979–1983*. London: Zed.

Federal Office of Statistics 1996. *Socio-Economic Profile of Nigeria*. Lagos: FOS.

Frynas, J. 1998. "Political Instability and Business: Focus on Shell in Nigeria", *Third World Quarterly*, Vol. 19, No. 3.

Garner, J. 1994. "No Minor Matter", *Index on Censorship*, 23, September–October.

Gbadamosi, G. 1992. "Development agency set up for oil states", *The Guardian*, July 11.

The Guardian. 1993. "An Unnecessary and Unhelpful Decree" (editorial), May 14.

— 1998. "Ijaw Leaders Dissociate from 'Kaiama Declaration'", December 30.

— 1999a. "ERA seeks release of Ijaw youth", January 4.

— 1999b. "Advertorial: The World Is Watching: Open Letter to All Oil Companies Operating in Nigeria", January 6.

Ghazi, P. and C. Duodu 1996. "How Shell tried to buy Berretas for Nigerians", *The Observer*, February 11.

Graf, W. 1988. *The Nigerian State: Political economy, state, class and political system in the post-colonial era*. London: James Currey.

"How Saro-Wiwa turned MOSOP into a Gestapo". 1985, np. (Anonymous anit-Saro-Wiwa Propaganda Pamphlet.)

Human Rights Watch 1999. *The Price of Oil, Corporate Responsibility and Human Rights Violations in Nigeria's Oil Producing Communities*. New York: Human Rights Watch.

Hutchful, E. 1985. "Oil Companies and Environmental Pollution in Nigeria", in Ake, Claude (ed.), *Political Economy of Nigeria*. London: Longmans Press.

Ibeanu, O. 1997. "Oil, Conflict and Security in Nigeria: Issues in the Ogoni Crisis", *AAPS Occasional Paper*, Vol. 1, No. 2.

— 1999. "Ogoni-oil, resource flow and conflict in rural Nigeria", in Granfelt, Tiiariita (ed.), *Managing the Globalised Environment*. London: IT Publications.

Ibrahim, J. 1993. "The Transition to Civil Rule: Sapping Democracy", in Olukoshi, Adebayo (ed.), *The Politics of Structural Adjustment in Nigeria*. London: James Currey.

Ihonvbere, J. 1991. "Structural Adjustment and Nigeria's Transition", *Trans Africa Forum*, Vol. 8, (3).

— 1993. "Economic Crisis, Structural Adjustment and Social Crisis in Nigeria", *World Development*, Vol. 31, No. 1.

— 1994. "The 'Irrelevant' State: Ethnicity and the Quest for Nationhood in Africa", *Ethnic and Racial Studies*, Vol. 17 (1).

Ihonvbere, J. and T. Shaw 1998. *Illusions of Power: Nigeria in Transition*. New Jersey: Africa World Press.

Ijaw Elders Forum 1999. Advertorial. "The Crisis in Ijaw (Izon) Land", *The Guardian*, January 15.

— 1999a Advertorial. "Burning Issues in Ijaw (Izon) Land. An Open Letter to General Abdulsalami Abubakar, GCFR, Mni, Head of State and Commander in Chief of the Armed Forces of Nigeria", published in *The Guardian*, April 25.

Ijaw National Congress 1999. Advertorial. "Reaction of the Ijaw National Congress (INC) to the Events that Followed the Kaiama Declaration", published in *The Guardian*, February 3.

Ijaw National Congress-USA n.d. "Fear God, Not Man: Choose Peace Not War". Open Letter to the Nigerian Head of State (His Excellency Gen. Abdulsalami Abubakar).

— 1998. Open Letter to the United Nations. 'Struggle for Self-Determination by the Oppressed Ijaw People of Nigeria: A Clarion Call for Global Support and International Recognition", New York, December 21.

— 1999a. "The Ijaw Struggle: News Update", January.

— 1999b. "Resolution of the Warri Crisis: The Historical Facts Must Not Be Ignored", Press Release, March 11.

Ikein, A. and C. Briggs-Anighoh 1998. *Oil and Fiscal Federalism: The Political Economy of Resource Allocation in a Developing Country*. Aldershot: Ashgate.

Ikwenze, C. 1999. "The Days of Rage in Yenagoa", *Vanguard*, January 3.

Ilenre, A. 1993. "The Ethnic Minority Question", *Nigeria Tribune*, November 1.

Inko-Tariah, O., J. Ahaiakwo, B. Alamina and G. Amadi 1990. Report of the Commission of Inquiry into the Causes and Circumstances of the Disturbances that Occurred at Umuechem in the Etche Local Government Area of Rivers State in the Federal Republic of Nigeria.

Izeze, I. 1994. "Nigeria Loses N2.732 billion to Ogoni Crisis", *Daily Sunray*, February 3.

Kaemi, T. (ed.) 1982. *Isaac Boro: The Twelve Day Revolution*. Benin City: Udodo Umeh Publishers.

The Kaiama Declaration 1998. Being the Communiqué Issued at the End of the All Ijaw Youth Conference, which was held in the Town of Kaiama, This 11Th Day of December, 1998.

Khan, S. 1994. *Nigeria: The political economy of oil*. Oxford: Oxford University Press.

Kpone-Tonwe, S. 1997. "Property Reckoning and Methods of Accumulating Wealth among the Ogoni of Eastern Niger Delta", *Africa*, 67 (1).

Kretzman, S. 1995. "Nigeria's Drilling Fields: Shell's Role in Repression", *Multinational Monitor*, 16, January–February.

Lewis, P. 1996. "Blood and oil: A special report, after Nigeria represses, Shell defends record", *New York Times International*, February, 13.

Laakso, L. and A. Olukoshi 1996. "The Crisis of the Post-Colonial Nation-State Project in Africa", in Olukoshi, Adebayo and Liisa Laakso (eds), *Challenges to the Nation-State in Africa*. Uppsala and Helsinki: The Nordic Africa Institute and the Institute of Development Studies.

Lijphart, A. 1977. *Democracy in Plural Societies: A Comparative Explanation*. New Haven and London: Yale University Press.

Lonsdale, J. 1996. "Moral Ethnicity and Political Tribalism", in Kaarsholm, Preben and Jan Hultin (eds), *Inventions and Boundaries: Historical and Anthropological Approaches to the Study of Ethnicity and Nationalism*. Roskilde: International Development Studies.

Loolo, G. 1981. *A History of the Ogoni*. Port Harcourt.

Lukula, T. 1993. "Ogonis Boycott Election", *The Guardian on Sunday*, June 13.

— 1994. "Oil Firms Count Losses, Proffer Solutions to Community Agitation", *The Guardian*, January 25.

Maier, K. 1993. "... as oil spill fuels Nigerian rivalries", *The Independent on Sunday*, August 15.

McGreal, C. 1993. "Spilt oil brews up a political storm", *The London Guardian*, August 11.

Moffat, D. and O. Linden 1995. "Perception and reality: assessing priorities for sustainable development in the Niger delta", *Ambio*, Vol. 24, No. 7–8, December.

MOSOP n.d. "The Ogoni Tragedy: An Appeal to the International Community".

— 1992. "Ogoni Bill of Rights", presented to the Government and People of Nigeria, October 1990. Port Harcourt: Saros International.

— 1993a. Press Statement. "Chief Philip Asiodu: The Nemesis of Oil Producing Areas".

—1993b. Press Statement. "Attack on Ogoni Life and Property in Nigeria", Port Harcourt, December 16.

— 1994. "Memorandum on the Ogoni Situation", presented to the Visiting Ministerial Team of Mr Donald Etiebet (Petroleum Resources), Chief Michael Ibru (Internal Affairs), and Chief Melford Okilo (Commerce and Tourism), January.

— 1994. Briefing Note. "Genocide in Ogoniland in the Niger Delta", April.

— 1996. "Briefing notes on events in Ogoni since the November 10 1995 executions", prepared for the Commonwealth Ministerial Action Group, London, MOSOP (UK), November 15.

— 1998. Press Release. "Ogoni Prisoners Accuse Shell's Private Police of Torture", May 10.
— 1999. News Release. "The Ogoni Twenty Are Now Free! Now All Ogoni People Must Be Free! We Need Your Support Now! September 20.
Mustapha, A. 1986. "The National Question and Radical Politics in Nigeria", *Review of African Political Economy*, 37, December.
Na' Allah, A. (ed.) 1998. *Ogoni's Agonies: Ken Saro-Wiwa and the Crisis in Nigeria*. New Jersey: Africa World Press.
Naanen, B. 1995. "Oil-Producing Minorities and the Restructuring of Nigerian Federalism: The Case of the Ogoni People", *Journal of Commonwealth and Comparative Politics*, Vol. 33, No. 1, March.
Naanen, B. and A. Pepple 1989. "State Movements", in Allagoa, E. and T. Tamuno (eds), *Land and People of Nigeria: Rivers State*. Port Harcourt: Riverside Communications.
National Concord 1999. "Riot Act for Niger Delta", January 1.
ND-HERO 1998a. Report. "Over 20,000 Women of Egi (in Rivers State) Protest against Elf Petroleum Development Company of Nigeria", November 23 and 24.
— 1998b. "Field Report of Looming Niger Delta Crisis", December 30.
— 1999. News Brief. "Soldiers under the Control of Agip Open Fire on Villagers, Killing 8, Arresting 2, and Chasing Away Other Villagers", April 22.
Newswatch 1993. "Exploitation: Agony of the Ogoni", January 25.
Niger Delta Wetlands Centre 1999. "Brief on Niger Delta: Nigeria", February.
Ngemutu-Roberts, F.O. 1994. "Federalism, minorities and political contestation in Nigeria: From Henry Willink to the MOSOP Phenomenon", paper presented to the Twentieth Nigerian Political Science Association Conference, Ile-Ife, February 28–March 2.
Niboro, I. 1997. "Shell's Racism in the Delta", *Tell*, August 12.
Niger Delta Alert, Vol. 1, No. 1
NigeriaNews.net 1999a. "Abubakar visits Ogoniland", April 30.
— 1999b. "Ijaw Youths Arrested", May 12.
Nnoli, O. 1978. *Ethnic Politics in Nigeria*. Enugu: Fourth Dimension Publishers.
— 1994. *Ethnicity and Democracy in Africa: Intervening Variables*. Lagos: Malthouse.
— 1995. *Ethnicity and Development in Nigeria*. Aldershot: Avebury.
Obi, C. 1995. "Oil Minority Rights versus the Nigerian State: Environmental Conflict, Its Implications and Transcendence", paper presented at CODESRIA's Eighth General Assembly and Conference, June 26–July 2.
Obi, C. 1997a. 'Globalisation and Local Resistance: The case of the Ogoni versus Shell', *New Political Economy*, Vol. 2, No. 1.
— 1997b. *Oil, Environmental Conflict and National Security: Ramifications of the Ecology-Security Nexus for Sub-Regional Peace*, ACDIS Occasional Paper, University of Illinois at Urbana Champaign.
— 1997c. *Structural Adjustment, Oil and Popular Struggles: The Deepening Crisis of State Legitimacy in Nigeria*. CODESRIA Monograph Series. Dakar: CODESRIA.
— 1998a. "Global, State and Local Intersections: A Study of Power, Authority and Conflict in the Niger Delta Oil Communities", paper presented at the Workshop on Local Governance and International Intervention, Florence, March 28–29.
— 1998b. "The Impact of Oil on Nigeria's Revenue Allocation System: Problems and Prospects for National Reconstruction", in Kunle Amuwo, et al. (eds), *Federalism and Political Restructuring in Nigeria*. Ibadan: Spectrum Books and IFRAA.

— 1998c. "The Changing Forms of Identity Politics in Nigeria under Economic Adjustment: The Case of the Oil Minorities of the Niger Delta". Research Proposal for the Nordic Africa Institute's Guest Researcher Scholarship Programme.

— 1998d. "Structural Adjustment and the Crisis of Environmental Governance in Nigeria". Unpublished report, Afrika Studiecentrum, Leiden, August.

— 1999. "Globalisation and Environmental Conflict in Africa", *African Journal of Political Science (New Series)*, Vol. 4, No. 1, June.

Obi, C. and K. Soremekun 1995. "Oil and the Nigerian State: An Overview", in Kayode Soremekun (ed.), *Perspectives on the Nigerian Oil Industry*. Lagos: Amkra Books.

Obibi, C. 1999a. "Ijaw women protest troops deployment to Bayelsa", *The Guardian*, January 12.

— 1999b. "Wages of a Siege", *The Guardian*, January 15.

— 1999c. "Beyond the security siege on Ijawland", *The Guardian*, January 18.

Ofuoku, M. 1998. "Why They Seethe", *Newswatch*, Vol. 28, No.18.

— 1999. "The Bomb Is Ticking", *Newswatch*, May 25.

Ogefere, S. 1999. "Our scorecard, by govt", *The Guardian*, May 13.

Ogele 1999. *Bulletin of the Ijaw Youth Congress*, No. 2.

Ogoni Patriotic Union 1994. "Memo to General Sanni Abacha", June 14.

Ogoni Study Group n.d. "Crisis in the Ogoniland—The true story", n.p.

Okafor, C. 1999a. "Isoko youth end siege on Shell stations", *The Guardian*, January 18.

— 1999b "Monarchs seek withdrawal of troops from oil producing areas", *The Guardian*, March 18.

Okpu, U. 1977. *Ethnic Minority Problems in Nigerian Politics: 1960–1965*, Uppsala: Studia Historica Upsaliensa.

Ollor-Obari, J. 1998a. "Ijaws Parallel Army", *The Guardian*, December 6.

— 1998b. "Invaders of oil installations to be treated as terrorists, says administrator", *The Guardian*, December 12.

— 1998c. "Ijaw seek control of oil resources", *The Guardian*, December 14.

— 1998d. "Oil workers, military get ultimatum to leave Ijaw area', *The Guardian*, December 16.

— 1998e. "Groups want speedy response to Niger delta problems", *The Guardian*, December, 25.

— 1998f. "State of Emergency in Bayelsa, Ijaw Youth Protest", *The Guardian*, December 31.

— 1999a. "Death toll in Yenagoa protest now seven", *The Guardian*, January 1.

— 1999b. "Govt deploys warships, troops in Bayelsa", *The Guardian*, January 4.

— 1999c. "Ijaw youths adamant as Bayelsa seeks truce", *The Guardian*, January 20.

— 1999d. "Bayelsa holds rulers liable for illegal meetings', *The Guardian*, January 22.

— 1999e. 'Why Niger Delta Crisis Festers, by Ijaw Leaders", *The Guardian*, January 28.

— 1999f. "Ijaw youths write Carter, allege military build-up in Niger Delta", *The Guardian*, March 9.

— 1999g. "MOSOP Faults Niger Delta Panel's Proposals", *The Guardian*, April 27.

— 1999h. "MOSOP criticises Commonwealth team's decision on Nigeria", *The Guardian*, May 5.

— 1999i. "MOSOP Demonstrates, Shell, Ogoni Leaders Meet", *The Guardian*, May 8.

Ollor-Obari, J. and E. Ezomon 1999. "Bayelsa Lifts Curfew, Ijaw Youths Call for Truce", *The Guardian*, January 5.

Ollor-Obari J. and C. Okafor 1999. "Govt's moves in Niger Delta, recipe for disaster, says MOSOP", *The Guardian*, March 9.

Olufemi, B. 1999. "Ijaw youth reject panel's recommendations", *The Guardian*, April 5.

Olufemi, B. and Ibiba Don-Pedro 1999. "We Want Justice in the Niger Delta", interview with Oronto Douglas, *The Guardian*, April 3.

Olufemi, B. and J. Ollor-Obari 1999. "ERA urges repeal of land use decree", *The Guardian*, May 31.

Olukoshi, A. (ed.) 1990. *Nigeria's External Debt Crisis: Its Management*. Lagos: Malthouse.

Olukoshi, A. 1993. *The Politics of Structural Adjustment in Nigeria*. London: James Currey.

— 1995. "Guilty Through and Through: Shell and the Plight of the Ogoni People", *Review of African Political Economy*, Vol. 22, Issue 66, December.

— 1997. "Associational Life", in Diamond, L., A. Kirk-Greene and Oyeleye Oyediran (eds), *Transition without End: Nigerian Politics and Civil Society under Babangida*. Ibadan: Vantage Publishers.

— 1998a. "Economic Crisis, Multipartyism and Opposition Politics in Contemporary Africa", in Olukoshi, Adebayo (ed.), *The Politics of Opposition in Contemporary Africa*, Uppsala: The Nordic Africa Institute.

— 1998b. *The Elusive Prince of Denmark: Structural Adjustment and the Crisis of Governance in Africa*. Research report no. 104. Uppsala: The Nordic Africa Institute.

— 1999. "State, Conflict and Democracy: The Complex Process of Renewal", in Richard Joseph (ed.), *State, Conflict and Democracy in Africa*. Boulder and London: Lynne Rienner Publishers.

Olukoshi, A. and A. Agbu 1996. "The Deepening Crisis of Nigerian Federalism and the Future of the Nation-state", in Olukoshi, Adebayo and Liisa Laakso (eds), *Challenges to the Nation-State in Africa*. Uppsala and Helsinki: The Nordic Africa Institute and the Institute of Development Studies.

Olukoshi, A. and C. Nwoke (eds) 1994. "The Theoretical and Conceptual Underpinnings of Structural Adjustment Programmes", in Olukoshi, Adebayo et al. (eds), *Structural Adjustment in West Africa*. Lagos: NIIA and Pumark.

Olumhense, S. 1993. "Your Money and Your Life", *Tell*, February 1.

Omoweh, D. 1994. "The Role of Shell Petroleum Development Corporation and the State in the Underdevelopment of the Niger Delta", Ph.D. Dissertation, Department of International Relations, Obafemi Awolowo University, Ile-Ife.

— 1996. "Environment and Poverty in the Oil Producing Areas of Nigeria", paper presented at the 1996 Annual Meeting of the Association of Third World Studies, Troy State University, Montgomery, Alabama.

Onanuga, B. 1998. "The Dangerous Oil Fields", *The News*, September 14.

Onuorah, M. and H. Oliomogbe 1999. "Groups seek troops withdrawal from Bayelsa", *The Guardian*, January 18.

Orage, D. 1998. "The Ogoni Question and the Role of the International Community in Nigeria", in Na' Allah, A. (ed.), *Ogoni's Agonies: Ken Saro-Wiwa and the Crisis in Nigeria*. New Jersey: Africa World Press.

Osaghae, E. 1991. "Ethnic Minorities and Federalism in Nigeria", *African Affairs*, 90.

— 1995a. "The Ogoni Uprising: Oil Politics, Minority Agitation and the Future of the Federal State", *African Affairs*, 94.

— 1995b. *Structural Adjustment and Ethnicity in Nigeria*. Research report no. 98. Uppsala: The Nordic Africa Institute.

— 1996. "Human Rights and Ethnic Conflict Management: The Case of Nigeria", *Journal of Peace Research*, Vol. 33, (2).
— 1998. "Managing Multiple Minority Problems in Nigeria", *Journal of Modern African Studies*, Vol. 36, No. 1.
Osunde, M. 1999a. "Ijaw Youth Council dissociates from pact with Obasanjo", *The Guardian*, January 5.
— 1999b. "Ijaw youth allege detention of 84 colleagues", *The Guardian*, January 30.
Otite, O. 1990. *Ethnic Pluralism and Ethnicity in Nigeria*. Ibadan: Shaneson.
Oyediran, O. (ed.) 1996. *Governance and Development in Nigeria: Essays in honour of Professor Billy J. Dudley*. Ibadan: Oyediran Consult.
Panter-Brick, S. (ed.) 1978. *Soldiers and Oil: The Political Transformation of Nigeria*. London: Frank Cass.
Pearson, Scott 1970. *Petroleum and the Nigerian Economy*. California: Stanford University Press.
Phillips, A. 1991. "Four decades of fiscal federalism in Nigeria", *PUBLIUS*, 21 (4), fall.
Phillips, A. and E. Ndekwu (eds) 1987. *Structural Adjustment in a Developing Economy: The case of Nigeria*. Ibadan: NISER.
Project Underground 1999. "Crackdown on Oil Protesters in the Niger Delta", *Drillbits and Tailings*, January 7.
Rabuska, A. and K. Stepsle 1972. *Politics in Plural Societies: A Theory of Political Instability*. Ohio: Charles E. Merril.
Reuters 1998. "State of Emergency Declared in Niger Delta Because of Non-Violent Protests Against Big Oil", December 31.
Rimmer, D. 1978. "Elements of Political Economy", in Panter-Brick, S. (ed.), *Soldiers and Oil: The Political Transformation of Nigeria*. London: Frank Cass.
Robinson, D. 1996. *Ogoni: The Struggle Continues*. Geneva and Nairobi: World Council of Churches and All African Council of Churches.
Rowell, A. 1994. *Shell-shocked: The environmental and social costs of living with Shell in Nigeria*. Amsterdam: Greenpeace International.
— 1996. "A Shell-shocked Land", in Rowell, Andrew, *Green Backlash: Global Subversion of the Environmental Movement*. London and New York: Routledge.
Sorunke, L. 1994. "Ogoni Protests Claim 1000 Lives", *Sunday Concord*, March 13.
Saro-Wiwa, K. 1968. *The Ogoni Nation today and tomorrow*. Port Harcourt: Saros International.
— 1989. *On a Darkling Plain*. Port Harcourt: Saros International.
— 1992. *Genocide in Nigeria: The Ogoni Tragedy*. London, Lagos and Port Harcourt: Saros International.
—. 1993. Quoted by Emmanual Efeni, "A Dance of Protest," *The Guardian* (Lagos), January 16.
— 1994a. *Ogoni Moment of Truth*. Port Harcourt: Saros International.
— 1994b. "Oil and the Basic Issues at Stake", *The Guardian*, April 1.
— 1995. *A Month and a Day: A Detention Diary*. London: Penguin Books.
Shell International Petroleum Corporation 1992. *Shell and the Environment*. London: SIPC.
— 1994. "Shell Briefing Note", London, SIPC Press Release, May.
— 1995. "Clear Thinking in Troubled Times", London, SIPC Press Release, November 19.
Shell Petroleum Development Corporation 1993. *Nigeria and Shell: Partners in Progress*. Lagos: SPDC.

Skogley, S. 1997. "Complexities in Human Rights Protection: Actors and Rights Involved in the Ogoni Conflict in Nigeria", *Netherlands Quarterly of Human Rights*, Vol. 15, No. 1.

Soremekun, K. and C. Obi 1993a. "The Changing Pattern of Private Foreign Investments in the Nigerian Oil Industry", *Africa Development*, Vol. XVIII, No. 3.

— 1993b. "Oil and the National Question", proceedings of the 1993 Nigerian Economic Society Annual Conference, Ibadan.

Sorunke, L. 1994. "Ogoni Protests Claim 1000 Lives", *Sunday Concord*, March 13.

Soyinka, W. 1996. *The Open Sore of a Continent: A personal narrative of the Nigerian Crisis.* New York: Oxford University Press.

Suberu, R. 1993. "The Travails of Federalism in Nigeria", *Journal of Democracy*, Vol. 4, No. 4, October.

— 1996. *Ethnic Minority Conflicts and Governance in Nigeria.* Ibadan: Spectrum and IFRAA.

Sunday Sketch 1993. "Ogonis Boycott', June 13.

Tamuno, T. 1970. "Separatist Agitation in Nigeria since 1914", *Journal of Modern African Studies*, 8 (4).

Tell 1994. "This Is Genocide", January 31,

Toby, A. 1992. "Structural Adjustment and Economic Development in Nigeria", *Indian Journal of African Studies*, Vol. V, No. 1.

Turner, L. 1978. *Oil Companies in the International System.* London: George Allen and Unwin.

Udogu, I. 1994. "The Allurement of Ethno-Nationalism in Nigerian Politics: The Contemporary Debate", *Journal of Asian and African Studies*, Vol. XXIX (3–4).

— 1997. *Nigeria and the Politics of Survival as a Nation-State.* Lewiston, Queenston, Lampeter: The Edwin Mellon Press.

Unrepresented Nations and Peoples Organisation 1994. "Arrested Ogoni Leaders Reject Nigerian Government Accusations", May 24.

Vanguard 1999. "Itsekiri leaders flay '99 budget", January 4.

Watts, M. 1994. "Oil as Money: The Devil's Excrement and the Spectacle of Black Gold", in Corbridge, S., R. Martin and N. Thrift (eds), *Money, Power and Space.* Oxford: Basic Blackwell.

Welch, C. 1995. "The Ogoni and Self-Determination: Increasing violence in Nigeria", *The Journal of Modern African Studies*, 33 (4).

Wright, S. 1998. *Nigeria: Struggle for Stability and Status.* Boulder: Westview Press.

Appendix 1

THE KAIAMA DECLARATION
BEING THE COMMUNIQUÉ ISSUED AT THE END OF THE ALL IYAW YOUTHS CONFERENCE WHICH WAS HELD IN THE TOWN OF KAIAMA THIS 11TH DAY OF DECEMBER 1998.

Introduction

We, Ijaw youths drawn from over five hundred communities from over 40 clans that make up the Ijaw nation and representing 25 representative organisations met, today, in Kaiama to deliberate on the best way to ensure the continuous survival of the indigenous peoples of the Ijaw ethnic nationality of the Niger Delta within the Nigerian state.

After exhaustive deliberations, the Conference observed:

a. That it was through British colonisation that the IJAW NATION was forcibly put under the Nigerian state.

b. That but for the economic interests of imperialists, the Ijaw ethnic nationality would have evolved as a distinct and separate sovereign nation, enjoying undiluted political, economic, social, and cultural AUTONOMY.

c. That the division of the Southern protectorate into the East and West in 1939 by the British marked the beginning of the balkanisation of a hitherto territorially contiguous and culturally homogenous Ijaw people into political and administrative units much to our disadvantage. This trend is continuing in the balkanisation of the Ijaws into six states—Ondo, Edo, Delta, Bayelsa, Rivers and Akwa Ibom States, mostly as minorities who suffer socio-political, cultural and psychological deprivations.

d. The quality of life of Ijaw people is deteriorating as a result of utter neglect, suppression and marginalisation visited on Ijaws by the alliance of the Nigerian State and transnational oil companies.

e. That the political crisis in Nigeria is mainly about the struggle for the control of oil mineral resources which account for over 80% of GDP, 95% of national budget and 90% of foreign exchange earnings. Despite these huge contributions, our reward from the Nigerian State remains avoidable deaths resulting from ecological devastation and military repression.

f. That the unabating damage done to our fragile natural environment and to the health of our people is due in the main to uncontrolled exploration and exploitation of crude oil and natural gas which has led to numerous oil spillages, uncontrolled gas flaring, the opening up of our forests to loggers, indiscriminate canalisation, flooding, land subsidence, coastal erosion, earth tremors etc. Oil and gas are exhaustible resources and the complete lack of concern for ecological rehabilitation, in the light of the Oloibiri experience, is a signal of impending doom for the peoples of Ijawland.

g. That the degradation of the environment of Ijawland by transnational oil companies and the Nigerian State arises mainly because Ijaw people have been robbed of their natural rights to ownership and control of their land and resources through the instrumentality of undemocratic Nigerian State legislations such as the Land Use Decree of 1978, the Petroleum Decrees of 1969 and 1991, the Lands (Title Vesting etc) Decree No. 52 of 1993 (Osborne Land Decree), the Inland Waterways Authority Decree No. 13 of 1997 etc.

h. That the principle of Derivation in Revenue Allocation has been consciously and systematically obliterated by successive regimes of the Nigerian State. We note the drastic reduction of the Derivation Principle from 100% (1953), 50% (1960), 45% (1970), 20% (1975), 2% (1982), 1.5% (1984), to 3% (1992 to date), and the rumoured 13% in Abacha's 1995 undemocratic and unimplemented constitution,

i. That the violence in Ijawland and other parts of the Niger Delta area, sometimes manifesting in intra- and inter-ethnic conflicts are sponsored by the State and transnational oil companies to keep the communities of the Niger Delta area divided, weak and distracted from the causes of their problems.

j. That the recent revelations of the looting of the national treasury by the Abacha junta is only a reflection of an existing and continuing trend of stealing by public office holders in the Nigerian state. We remember the over 12 billion dollars Gulf war windfall, which was looted by Babangida and his cohorts. We note that over 70% of the billions of dollars being looted by military rulers and their civilian collaborators is derived from our ecologically devastated Ijawland.

Based on the foregoing, we, the youths of Ijawland hereby make the following resolutions to be known as the Kaiama Declaration:

All land and natural resources (including mineral resources) within the Ijaw territory belong to Ijaw communities and are the basis of our survival.

We cease to recognise all undemocratic decrees that rob our peoples/communities of the right to ownership and control of our lives and resources, which were enacted without our participation and consent. These include the Land Use Decree and the Petroleum Decree.

We demand the immediate withdrawal from Ijawland of all military forces of occupation and repression by the Nigerian State. Any oil company that employs the services of the armed forces of the Nigerian state to "protect" its operations will be viewed as an enemy of the Ijaw people. Family members of military personnel stationed in Ijawland should appeal to their people to leave the Ijaw area alone.

Ijaw youths in all the communities in all Ijaw clans in the Niger Delta will take steps to implement these resolutions beginning from the 30th of December, 1998, as a step towards reclaiming the control of our lives. We, therefore, demand that all oil companies stop all exploration and exploitation activities in the Ijaw area. We are tired of gas flaring, oil spillages, blowouts and being labelled saboteurs and terrorists. It is a case of preparing the noose for our hanging. We reject this labelling. Hence we advise all oil companies staff and contractors to withdraw from Ijaw territories by the 30th of December, 1998 pending the resolution of the issue of resource ownership and control in the Ijaw area of the Niger Delta.

Ijaw youths and Peoples will promote the principle of peaceful coexistence between all Ijaw communities and with immediate neighbours, despite the provocative and divisive actions of the Nigerian State, transnational oil companies and their contractors. We offer the hand of friendship and comradeship to our neighbours: the Itsekiri, Ilaje, Urhobo, Isoko, Edo, Ibibio, Ogoni, Ekpeye, Ikwerre etc. We affirm our commitment to joint struggle with the other ethnic nationalities of the Niger Delta for self-determination.

We express solidarity with all peoples organisations and ethnic nationalities in Nigeria and elsewhere who are struggling for self-determination and justice. In particular we note the struggle of the Oodua Peoples Congress (OPC), the Movement for the Survival of Ogoni People (MOSOP), Egi Women's Movement etc.

We extend our hand of solidarity to the Nigerian oil workers (**NUPENG and PENGASSAN**) and expect that they will see this struggle for freedom as a struggle for humanity,

We reject the present transition to civil rule programme of the Abubakar regime, as it is not preceded by restructuring of the Nigerian federation. The way forward is a Sovereign National Conference of equally represented ethnic nationalities to discuss the nature of a democratic federation of Nigerian ethnic nationalities. Conference noted the violence and killings that characterised the last local government elections in most parts of the Niger Delta. Conference pointed out that these electoral conflicts are a manifestation of the undemocratic and unjust nature of the military transition programme. Conference affirmed therefore, that the military are incapable of enthroning true democracy in Nigeria.

We call on all Ijaws to remain true to their Ijawness and to work for the total liberation of our people. You have no other true home but that which is in Ijawland.

We agreed to remain within Nigeria but to demand and work for self-government and resource control for Ijaw people. Conference approved that the best way for Nigeria is a federation of ethnic nationalities. The federation should be run on the basis of equality and social justice.

Finally, Ijaw youths resolve to set up the Ijaw Youth Council (IYC) to coordinate the struggle of Ijaw peoples for self-determination and justice.

Signed for the Entire Participants

Felix Tuodolo

Ogoriba, Timi Kaiser-Wihlelm

Appendix 2

OGONI BILL OF RIGHTS
PRESENTED TO THE GOVERNMENT AND PEOPLE OF NIGERIA

We, the people of Ogoni (Babbe, Gokanna, Ken Khana, Nyo Khana and Tai) numbering about 500,000 being a separate and distinct ethnic nationality within the Federal Republic of Nigeria, wish to draw the attention of the Government and people of Nigeria to the undermentioned facts:

1. That the Ogoni people, before the advent of British colonialism, were not conquered or colonised by any other ethnic group in present day Nigeria.
2. That British colonisation forced us into the administrative division of Opobo from 1908 to 1947.
3. That we protested against this forced union until the Ogoni Native Authority was created in 1947 and placed under the then Rivers Province.
4. That in 1951 we were forcibly included in the Eastern Region of Nigeria where we suffered utter neglect.
5. That we protested against this neglect by voting against the party in power in the region in 1957, and against the forced union by the testimony before the Willink Commission of Inquiry into Minority Fears in 1958.
6. That this protest led to the inclusion of our nationality in Rivers state in 1967, which state consists of several ethnic nationalities with differing cultures, languages and aspirations.
7. That oil was struck and produced in commercial quantities on our land in 1958 at K. Dere (Bomu oilfield).
8. That oil has been mined on our land since 1958 to this day from the following oilfields: (I) Bomu (ii) Bodo West (iii) Tai (iv) Korokoro (v) Yorla (vi) Lubara Creek and (vii) Afam by Shell Petroleum Development Company (Nigeria) Limited.
9. That in over 30 years of oil mining, the Ogoni nationality have provided the Nigerian nation over 40 billion Naira (N40 billion) or 30 billion dollars.
10. That in return for the above contribution, the Ogoni people have received NOTHING.
11. That today, the Ogoni people have: (I) No representation whatsoever in ALL institutions of the Federal Government of Nigeria. (ii) No pipe-borne water. (iii) No electricity. (iv) No job opportunities for the citizens in the Federal, State, public sector or private companies.
12. That the Ogoni languages of Gokana and Khana are undeveloped and are about to disappear, whereas other Nigerian languages are being forced on us.
13. That the ethnic politics of successive Federal and State Governments are gradually pushing the Ogoni to slavery and possible extinction.

14. That the Shell Petroleum Development Company of Nigeria Limited does not employ Ogoni people at a meaningful or any level at all, in defiance of the Federal government's regulations.
15. That the search for oil has caused severe land and food shortages in Ogoni one of the most densely populated areas of Africa (average: 1,500 per square mile; Nigerian national average: 300 per square mile).
16. That the neglectful environmental pollution laws and sub-standard inspection techniques of the Federal authorities have led to the complete degradation of the Ogoni environment, turning our homeland into an ecological disaster.
17. That the Ogoni people lack education, health and other social facilities.
18. That it is intolerable that one of the richest areas of Nigeria should wallow in abject poverty and destitution.
19. That successive Federal administrations have trampled on every minority right enshrined in the Nigerian Constitution to the detriment of the Ogoni and have by administrative structuring and other noxious acts transferred Ogoni wealth exclusively to other parts of the Republic.
20. That the Ogoni people wish to manage their own affairs.

Now, therefore, while reaffirming our wish to remain a part of the Federal Republic of Nigeria, we make demand upon the Republic as follows:

That the Ogoni people be granted **POLITICAL AUTONOMY** to participate in the affairs of the Republic as a distinct and separate unit by whatever name it is called, provided that this Autonomy guarantees the following:

(a) Political control of Ogoni affairs by Ogoni people.

(b) The right to the control and use of a fair proportion of Ogoni economic resources for Ogoni development.

(c) Adequate and direct representation as of right in all Nigerian national institutions.

(d) The use and development of Ogoni languages in Ogoni territory.

(e) The full development of Ogoni culture.

(f) The right to religious freedom.

(g) The right to protect the Ogoni environment and ecology from further degradation.

We make the above demand in the knowledge that it does not deny any other ethnic group in the Nigerian Federation of their rights and that it can only conduce to peace, justice and fairplay and hence stability and progress in the Nigerian nation.

We make the above demand in the belief that, as Obafemi Awolowo has written:

In a true federation, each ethnic group no matter how small, is entitled to the same treatment as any other ethnic group, no matter how large.

We demand these rights as equal members of the Nigerian federation who contribute and have contributed to the growth of the Federation and have a right to expect full returns from that Federation.

Adopted by general acclaim of the Ogoni People on the 26th day of August, 1990 at Bori, Rivers State.

Signed on behalf of the Ogoni people by:

Babbe: Sgd. HRH Mark Tsaro-Igbara, Gbenemene Babbe; HRH F.M.K. Noryaa, Menebua Ka-Babbe; Chief M.A.M. Tornwe III, JP; Prince J.S. Sangha; Dr Israel Kue; Chief A.M.N. Gua.

Gokana: Sgd. HRH James P. Bagia Gberesako XI, Gberemene Gokana; HRH C.A. Mitee, JP, Menebua Numuu; Chief E.N. Kobani, JP, Tonsimene Gokana; Dr B.N. Birabi, Chief Kemte Giadom, JP; Chief S.N. Orage.

Nyo-Khana: Sgd. HRH W.ZP. Nzidee, Gbenemene Baa I of Nyo-Khana; Dr G.B. Leton, OON JP; Mr Lekue Lah Loolo; Mr L.E. Mwara; Chief E.A. Apenu; Pastor M.P. Maeba.

Ken-Khana: Sgd. HRH M. H.S. Eguru, Gbenemene Ken Khana; HRH C.B.S. Nwikina-Emah III, Menebua Bom; Mr M. C. Daanwi; Chief T.N. Nwieke; Mr Ken Saro-Wiwa; Mr Simeon Idemyor.

Tai: Sgd. HRH B.A. Mballey, Gbenemene Tai; HRH G.N.K. Gininwa, Menebua Tua Tua; Chief J. S. Agbara; Chief D.J.K. Kumbe; Chief Fred Gwezia; HRH A. Demor-Kanni, Menebua Nonwa Tai.

Appendix 3

ADDENDUM TO THE OGONI BILL OF RIGHTS

We, the people of Ogoni, being a separate and distinct ethnic nationality within the Federal Republic of Nigeria, hereby state as follows:

A. That on October 2, 1990 we addressed an "Ogoni Bill of Rights" to the President of the Federal Republic of Nigeria, General Ibrahim Babangida and members of the Armed Forces Ruling Council;

B. That after a one-year wait, the President has been unable to grant us the audience which we sought to have with him in order to discuss the legitimate demands contained in the Ogoni Bill of Rights;

C. That our demands as outlined in the Ogoni Bill of Rights are legitimate, just and our inalienable right and in accord with civilised values worldwide;

D. That the Government of the Federal Republic has continued, since October 2, 1990, to decree measures and implement policies which further marginalise the Ogoni people, denying us political autonomy, our rights to our resources, to the development of our languages and culture, to adequate representation as of right in all Nigerian institutions and to the protection of our environment and ecology from further degradation;

That we cannot sit idly by while we are, as a people, dehumanized and slowly exterminated and driven to extinction even as our rich resources are siphoned off to the exclusive comfort and improvement of other Nigerian communities, and the shareholders of multinational oil companies.

Now, therefore, while re-affirming our wish to remain a part of the Federal Republic of Nigeria, we hereby authorise the Movement for the Survival of Ogoni People (MOSOP) to make representation, for as long as these injustices continue, to the United Nations Commission on Human Rights, the Commonwealth Secretariat, the African Commission on Human and Peoples' Rights, the European Community and all international bodies which have a role to play in the preservation of our nationality as follows:

1. That the Government of the Federal Republic of Nigeria has, in utter disregard and contempt for human rights, since independence in 1960 till date, denied us our political rights to self-determination, economic rights to our resources, cultural rights to the development of our languages and culture, and social rights to education, health and adequate housing and to representation as of right in national institutions;

2. That, in particular, the Federal Republic of Nigeria has refused to pay us oil royalties and mining rents amounting to an estimated 20 billion US dollars for petroleum mined from our soil for over thirty-five years;

3. That the Constitution of the Federal Republic of Nigeria does not protect any of our rights whatsoever as an ethnic minority of 500,000 in a nation of about 100 million people and that the voting power and military might of the majority ethnic groups have been remorselessly used against us at every point in time;

4. That multinational oil companies, namely Shell (Dutch and British) and Chevron (American) have severally and jointly devastated our environment and ecology, having flared gas in our villages for 33 years and caused oil spillages, blow outs etc, and have dehumanised our people, denying them employment and those benefits which industrial organisations in Europe and America routinely contribute to their areas of operation;

5. That the Nigerian elite (bureaucratic, military, industrial and academic) have turned a blind eye and a deaf ear to these acts of dehumanisation by the ethnic majority and have colluded with all the agents of destruction aimed at us;

6. That we cannot seek restitution in the courts of law in Nigeria as the act of expropriation of our rights and resources has been institutionalised in the 1979 and 1989 Constitutions of the Federal Republic of Nigeria, which constitutions were acts of a Constituent Assembly imposed by a military regime and do not, in any way, protect minority rights or bear resemblance to the tacit agreement made at Nigerian independence;

7. That the Ogoni people abjure violence in their just struggle for their rights within the Federal Republic of Nigeria but will, through every lawful means, and for as long as it is necessary, fight for the social justice and equity for themselves and their progeny, and in particular demand political autonomy as a distinct and separate unit within the Nigerian nation with full right to (i) control Ogoni political affairs (ii) use at least fifty per cent of Ogoni economic resources for Ogoni development (iii) protect the Ogoni environment and ecology from further degradation (iv) ensure the full restitution of the harm done to our people by the flaring of gas, oil spillages, oil blow outs, etc. by the following oil companies: Shell, Chevron and their Nigerian accomplices;

8. That without the intervention of the international community, the Government of the Federal Republic of Nigeria and the ethnic majority will continue these noxious policies until the Ogoni people are obliterated from the face of the earth.

Adopted by the general acclaim of the Ogoni people on the 26th day of August 1991 at Bori, Rivers state of Nigeria. Signed on behalf of the Ogoni people by:

Babbe: Sgd. HRH Mark Tsaro-Igbara, Gbenemene Babbe; HRH F.M.K. Noryaa, Menebua Ka-Babbe; Chief M.A. M. Tornwe III, JP; Prince J.S. Sangha; Dr Israel Kue; Chief A.M.N. Gua.

Gokana: Sgd. HRH James P. Bagia, Gberesako XI, Gberemene Gokana; Chief E.N. Kobani, JP; Tonsimene Gokana; Dr B.N. Birabi; Chief Kemte Giadom, JP; Chief S.N. Orage.

Nyo-Khana: Sgd. HRH W.Z.P. Nzidee, Gbenemene Baa 1 of Nyo-Khana; Dr G.B. Leton, OON, JP; Mr Lekue Lah Loloo; Mr L.E. Mwara; Chief E.A. Apenu; Pastor M.P. Maeba.

Ken-Khana: Sgd. HRH M.H.S. Eguru, Gbenemene Ken-Khana; HRH C.B.S. Nwikina-Emah III, Menebua Bom; Mr M.C. Daanwi; Chief T.N. Nwieke; Mr Ken Saro-Wiwa; Mr Simeon Idemyor.

Tai: Sgd. HRH B.A. Mballey, Gbenemene Tai; HRH G.N.K. Gininwa, Menebua Tua Tua; Chief J.S. Agbara; Chief D.J.K. Kumbe; Chief Fred Gwezia; HRH A. Demor-Kanni, Menebua Nonwa Tai.

Publications of the research programme "Political and Social Context of Structural Adjustment in Africa" published by the Nordic Africa Institute

Gibbon P., Bangura and A. Ofstad (eds.), 1992, *Authoritarianism, Democracy and Adjustment. The Politics of Economic Reform in Africa*. Seminar proceedings no. 26.

Gibbon, P. (ed.), 1993, *Social Change and Economic Reform in Africa*.

Chachage, C.S.L., M. Ericsson and P. Gibbon, 1993, *Mining and Structural Adjustment. Studies on Zimbabwe and Tanzania*. Research report no. 92.

Neocosmos, M., 1993, *The Agrarian Question in Africa and the Concept of "Accumulation from Below". Economics and Politics in the Struggle for Democracy*. Research report no. 93.

Kanyinga. K., A.S.Z. Kiondo and P. Tidemand, 1994, *The New Local Level Politics in East Africa. Studies on Uganda, Tanzania and Kenya*. Edited and introduced by Peter Gibbon. Research report no. 95.

Osaghae, E.E., 1995, *Structural Adjustment and Ethnicity in Nigeria*. Research report no. 98.

Gibbon, P. (ed.), 1995, *Markets, Civil Society and Democracy in Kenya*.

Gibbon P. (ed.), 1995, *Structural Adjustment and the Working Poor in Zimbabwe*.

Gibbon, P., 1995, *Liberalised Development in Tanzania*.

Bijlmakers. L.A., M.T. Bassett and D.M. Sanders, 1996, *Health and Structural Adjustment in Rural and Urban Zimbabwe*. Research report no. 101.

Gibbon, P. and A.O. Olukoshi, 1996, *Structural Adjustment and Socio-Economic Change in Sub-Saharan Africa. Some Conceptual, Methodological and Research Issues*. Research report no. 102.

Olukoshi. A.O. and L. Laakso (eds.), 1996, *Challenges to the Nation-State in Africa*.

Olukoshi, A.O. (ed.), 1998, *The Politics of Opposition in Contemporary Africa*.

Egwu, S.G., 1998, *Structural Adjustment, Agrarian Change and Rural Ethnicity in Nigeria*. Research report no. 103.

Olukoshi, A.O., 1998, *The Elusive Prince of Denmark. Structural Adjustment and the Crisis of Governance in Africa*. Research report no. 104.

Bijlmakers. L.A., M.T. Bassett and D.M. Sanders, 1998, *Socioeconomic Stress, Health and Child Nutritional Status in Zimbabwe at a Time of Economic Structural Adjustment. A Three Year Longitudinal Study*. Research report no. 105.

Mupedziswa, R. and P. Gumbo, 1998, *Structural Adjustment and Women Informal Sector Traders in Harare, Zimbabwe*. Research report no. 106.

Chiwele, D.K., P. Muyatwa-Sipula and H. Kalinda, 1998, *Private Sector Response to Agricultural Marketing Liberalisation in Zambia. A Case Study of Eastern Province Maize Markets*. Research report no. 107.

Amanor, K.S., 1999, *Global Restructuring and Land Rights in Ghana. Forest Food Chains, Timber and Rural Livelihoods*. Research report no. 108.

Ongile, G.A., 1999, *Gender and Agricultural Supply Responses to Structural Adjustment Programmes. A Case Study of Smallholder Tea Producers in Kericho, Kenya*. Research report no. 109.

Sachikonye, Lloyd M., 1999, *Restructuring or De-Industrializing? Zimbabwe's Textile and Metal Industries under Adjustment*. Research report no. 110.

Gaidzanwa, Rudo, 1999, *Voting with their Feet. Zimbabwean Nurses and Doctors in the Era of Structural Adjustment*. Research report no. 111.

Hashim, Yahaya and Kate Meagher, 1999, *Cross-Border Trade and the Parallel Currency Market—Trade and Finance in the Context of Structural Adjustment. A Case Study from Kano, Nigeria*. Research report no. 113.

Moyo, Sam, 2000, *Land Reform under Structural Adjustment in Zimbabwe. Land Use Change in the Mashonaland Provinces*.

Jega, Attahiru (ed.), 2000, *Identity Transformation and Identity Politics under Structural Adjustment in Nigeria*.

Kanyinga, Karuti, 2000, *Re-Distribution from Above. The Politics of Land Rights and Squatting in Coastal Kenya*. Research report no. 115.

Amanor, Kojo Sebastian, 2001, *Land, Labour and the Family in Southern Ghana. A Critique of Land Policy under Neo-Liberalisation*. Research report no. 116.

Mupedziswa, Rodreck and Perpetua Gumbo, 2001, *Women Informal Traders in Harare and the Struggle for Survival in an Environment of Economic Reforms*. Research report no. 117.

Obi, Cyril I., *The Changing Forms of Identity Politics in Nigeria under Economic Adjustment. The Case of the Oil Minorities Movement of the Niger Delta*. Research report no. 119.

Research Reports published by the Institute

Some of the reports are out of print. Photocopies of these reports can be obtained at a cost of SEK 0:50/page.

1. Meyer-Heiselberg, Richard, *Notes from Liberated African Department in the Archives at Fourah Bay College, Freetown, Sierra Leone*. 61 pp. 1967 (OUT-OF-PRINT)
2. Not published.
3. Carlsson, Gunnar, *Benthonic Fauna in African Watercourses with Special Reference to Black Fly Populations*. 13 pp. 1968 (OUT-OF-PRINT)
4. Eldblom, Lars, *Land Tenure—Social Organization and Structure*. 18 pp. 1969 (OUT-OF-PRINT)
5. Bjerén, Gunilla, *Makelle Elementary School Drop-Out. 1967*. 80 pp. 1969 (OUT-OF-PRINT)
6. Møberg, Jens Peter, *Report Concerning the Soil Profile Investigation and Collection of Soil Samples in the West Lake Region of Tanzania*. 44 pp. 1970 (OUT-OF-PRINT)
7. Selinus, Ruth, *The Traditional Foods of the Central Ethiopian Highlands*. 34 pp. 1971 (OUT-OF-PRINT)
8. Hägg, Ingemund, *Some State-Controlled Industrial Companies in Tanzania. A Case Study*. 18 pp. 1971 (OUT-OF-PRINT)
9. Bjerén, Gunilla, *Some Theoretical and Methodological Aspects of the Study of African Urbanization*. 38 pp. 1971 (OUT-OF-PRINT)
10. Linné, Olga, *An Evaluation of Kenya Science Teacher's College*. 67 pp. 1971. SEK 45,-
11. Nellis, John R., *Who Pays Tax in Kenya?* 22 pp. 1972. SEK 45,-
12. Bondestam, Lars, *Population Growth Control in Kenya*. 59 pp. 1972 (OUT OF PRINT)
13. Hall, Budd L., *Wakati Wa Furaha. An Evaluation of a Radio Study Group Campaign*. 47 pp. 1973. SEK 45,-
14. Ståhl, Michael, *Contradictions in Agricultural Development. A Study of Three Minimum Package Projects in Southern Ethiopia*. 65 pp. 1973 (OUT-OF-PRINT)
15. Linné, Olga, *An Evaluation of Kenya Science Teachers College. Phase II 1970–71*. 91 pp. 1973 (OUT-OF-PRINT)
16. Lodhi, Abdulaziz Y., *The Institution of Slavery in Zanzibar and Pemba*. 40 pp. 1973. ISBN 91-7106-066-9 (OUT-OF-PRINT)
17. Lundqvist, Jan, *The Economic Structure of Morogoro Town. Some Sectoral and Regional Characteristics of a Medium-Sized African Town*. 70 pp. 1973. ISBN 91-7106-068-5 (OUT-OF-PRINT)
18. Bondestam, Lars, *Some Notes on African Statistics. Collection, Reliability and Interpretation*. 59 pp. 1973. ISBN 91-7106-069-4 (OUT-OF-PRINT)
19. Jensen, Peter Føge, *Soviet Research on Africa. With Special Reference to International Relations*. 68 pp. 1973. ISBN 91-7106-070-7 (OUT-OF-PRINT)
20. Sjöström, Rolf & Margareta, *YDLC—A Literacy Campaign in Ethiopia. An Introductory Study and a Plan for Further Research*. 72 pp. 1973. ISBN 91-7106-071-5 (OUT-OF-PRINT)
21. Ndongko, Wilfred A., *Regional Economic Planning in Cameroon*. 21 pp. 1974. SEK 45,-. ISBN 91-7106-073-1
22. Pipping-van Hulten, Ida, *An Episode of Colonial History: The German Press in Tanzania 1901–1914*. 47 pp. 1974. SEK 45,-. ISBN 91-7106-077-4
23. Magnusson, Åke, *Swedish Investments in South Africa*. 57 pp. 1974. SEK 45,-. ISBN 91-7106-078-2
24. Nellis, John R., *The Ethnic Composition of Leading Kenyan Government Positions*. 26 pp. 1974. SEK 45,-. ISBN 91-7106-079-0
25. Francke, Anita, *Kibaha Farmers' Training Centre. Impact Study 1965–1968*. 106 pp. 1974. SEK 45,-. ISBN 91-7106-081-2
26. Aasland, Tertit, *On the Move-to-the-Left in Uganda 1969–1971*. 71 pp. 1974. SEK 45,-. ISBN 91-7106-083-9
27. Kirk-Greene, Anthony H.M., *The Genesis of the Nigerian Civil War and the Theory of Fear*. 32 pp. 1975. SEK 45,-. ISBN 91-7106-085-5
28. Okereke, Okoro, *Agrarian Development Programmes of African Countries. A Reappraisal of Problems of Policy*. 20 pp. 1975. SEK 45,-. ISBN 91-7106-086-3
29. Kjekshus, Helge, *The Elected Elite. A Socio-Economic Profile of Candidates in Tanzania's Parliamentary Election, 1970*. 40 pp. 1975. SEK 45,-. ISBN 91-7106-087-1
30. Frantz, Charles, *Pastoral Societies, Stratification and National Integration in Africa*. 34 pp. 1975. ISBN 91-7106-088-X (OUT OF PRINT)
31. Esh, Tina & Illith Rosenblum, *Tourism in Developing Countries—Trick or Treat? A Report from the Gambia*. 80 pp. 1975. ISBN 91-7106-094-4 (OUT-OF-PRINT)
32. Clayton, Anthony, *The 1948 Zanzibar General Strike*. 66 pp. 1976. ISBN 91-7106-094-4 (OUT OF PRINT)
33. Pipping, Knut, *Land Holding in the Usangu Plain. A Survey of Two Villages in the Southern Highlands of Tanzania*. 122 pp. 1976. ISBN 91-7106-097-9 (OUT OF PRINT)
34. Lundström, Karl Johan, *North-Eastern Ethiopia: Society in Famine. A Study of Three Social Institutions in a Period of Severe Strain*. 80 pp. 1976. ISBN 91-7106-098-7 (OUT-OF-PRINT)
35. Magnusson, Åke, *The Voice of South Africa*. 55 pp. 1976. ISBN 91-7106-106-1 (OUT OF PRINT)

36. Ghai, Yash P., *Reflection on Law and Economic Integration in East Africa*. 41 pp. 1976. ISBN 91-7106-105-3 (OUT-OF-PRINT)

37. Carlsson, Jerker, *Transnational Companies in Liberia. The Role of Transnational Companies in the Economic Development of Liberia*. 51 pp. 1977. SEK 45,-. ISBN 91-7106-107-X

38. Green, Reginald H., *Toward Socialism and Self Reliance. Tanzania's Striving for Sustained Transition Projected*. 57 pp. 1977. ISBN 91-7106-108-8 (OUT-OF-PRINT)

39. Sjöström, Rolf & Margareta, *Literacy Schools in a Rural Society. A Study of Yemissrach Dimts Literacy Campaign in Ethiopia*. 130 pp. 1977. ISBN 91-7106-109-6 (OUT-OF-PRINT)

40. Ståhl, Michael, *New Seeds in Old Soil. A Study of the Land Reform Process in Western Wollega, Ethiopia 1975–76*. 90 pp. 1977. SEK 45,-. ISBN 91-7106-112-6

41. Holmberg, Johan, *Grain Marketing and Land Reform in Ethiopia. An Analysis of the Marketing and Pricing of Food Grains in 1976 after the Land Reform*. 34 pp. 1977. ISBN 91-7106-113-4 (OUT-OF-PRINT)

42. Egerö, Bertil, *Mozambique and Angola: Reconstruction in the Social Sciences*. 78 pp. 1977. ISBN 91-7106-118-5 (OUT OF PRINT)

43. Hansen, H. B., *Ethnicity and Military Rule in Uganda*. 136 pp. 1977. ISBN 91-7106-118-5 (OUT-OF-PRINT)

44. Bhagavan, M.R., *Zambia: Impact of Industrial Strategy on Regional Imbalance and Social Inequality*. 76 pp. 1978. ISBN 91-7106-119-3 (OUT OF PRINT)

45. Aaby, Peter, *The State of Guinea-Bissau. African Socialism or Socialism in Africa?* 35 pp. 1978. ISBN 91-7106-133-9 (OUT-OF-PRINT)

46. Abdel-Rahim, Muddathir, *Changing Patterns of Civilian-Military Relations in the Sudan*. 32 pp. 1978. ISBN 91-7106-137-1 (OUT-OF-PRINT)

47. Jönsson, Lars, *La Révolution Agraire en Algérie. Historique, contenu et problèmes*. 84 pp. 1978. ISBN 91-7106-145-2 (OUT-OF-PRINT)

48. Bhagavan, M.R., *A Critique of "Appropriate" Technology for Underdeveloped Countries*. 56 pp. 1979. SEK 45,-. ISBN 91-7106-150-9

49. Bhagavan, M.R., *Inter-Relations Between Technological Choices and Industrial Strategies in Third World Countries*. 79 pp. 1979. SEK 45,-. ISBN 91-7106-151-7

50. Torp, Jens Erik, *Industrial Planning and Development in Mozambique. Some Preliminary Considerations*. 59 pp. 1979. ISBN 91-7106-153-3 (OUT-OF-PRINT)

51. Brandström, Per, Jan Hultin & Jan Lindström, *Aspects of Agro-Pastoralism in East Africa*. 60 pp. 1979. ISBN 91-7106-155-X (OUT OF PRINT)

52. Egerö, Bertil, *Colonization and Migration. A Summary of Border-Crossing Movements in Tanzania before 1967*. 45 pp. 1979. SEK 45,-. ISBN 91-7106-159-2

53. Simson, Howard, *Zimbabwe—A Country Study*. 138 pp. 1979. ISBN 91-7106-160-6 (OUT-OF-PRINT)

54. Beshir, Mohamed Omer, *Diversity Regionalism and National Unity*. 50 pp. 1979. ISBN 91-7106-166-5 (OUT-OF-PRINT)

55. Eriksen, Tore Linné, *Modern African History: Some Historiographical Observations*. 27 pp. 1979. ISBN 91-7106-167-3 (OUT OF PRINT)

56. Melander, Göran, *Refugees in Somalia*. 48 pp. 1980. SEK 45,-. ISBN 91-7106-169-X

57. Bhagavan, M.R., *Angola: Prospects for Socialist Industrialisation*. 48 pp. 1980. ISBN 91-7106-175-4 (OUT OF PRINT)

58. Green, Reginald H., *From Südwestafrika to Namibia. The Political Economy of Transition*. 45 pp. 1981. SEK 45,-. ISBN 91-7106-188-6

59. Isaksen, Jan, *Macro-Economic Management and Bureaucracy: The Case of Botswana*. 53 pp. 1981. SEK 45,-. ISBN 91-7106-192-4

60. Odén, Bertil, *The Macroeconomic Position of Botswana*. 84 pp. 1981. SEK 45,-. ISBN 91-7106-193-2

61. Westerlund, David, *From Socialism to Islam? Notes on Islam as a Political Factor in Contemporary Africa*. 62 pp. 1982. SEK 45,-. ISBN 91-7106-203-3

62. Tostensen, Arne, *Dependence and Collective Self-Reliance in Southern Africa. The Case of the Southern African Development Coordination Conference (SADCC)*. 170 pp. 1982. ISBN 91-7106-207-6 (OUT-OF-PRINT)

63. Rudebeck, Lars, *Problèmes de pouvoir populaire et de développement. Transition difficile en Guinée-Bissau*. 73 pp. 1982. ISBN 91-7106-208-4 (OUT-OF-PRINT)

64. Nobel, Peter, *Refugee Law in the Sudan. With The Refugee Conventions and The Regulation of Asylum Act of 1974*. 56 pp. 1982. SEK 45,-. ISBN 91-7106-209-2

65. Sano, H-O, *The Political Economy of Food in Nigeria 1960–1982. A Discussion on Peasants, State, and World Economy*. 108 pp. 1983. ISBN 91-7106-210-6 (OUT-OF-PRINT)

66. Kjærby, Finn, *Problems and Contradictions in the Development of Ox-Cultivation in Tanzania*. 164 pp. 1983. SEK 60,-. ISBN 91-7106-211-4

67. Kibreab, Gaim, *Reflections on the African Refugee Problem: A Critical Analysis of Some Basic Assumptions*. 154 pp. 1983. ISBN 91-7106-212-2 (OUT-OF-PRINT) (

68. Haarløv, Jens, *Labour Regulation and Black Workers' Struggles in South Africa*. 80 pp. 1983. SEK 20,-. ISBN 91-7106-213-0

69. Matshazi, Meshack Jongilanga & Christina Tillfors, *A Survey of Workers' Education Activities in Zimbabwe, 1980–1981*. 85 pp. 1983. SEK 45,-. ISBN 91-7106-217-3

70. Hedlund, Hans & Mats Lundahl, *Migration and Social Change in Rural Zambia*. 107 pp. 1983. SEK 50,-. ISBN 91-7106-220-3

71. Gasarasi, Charles P., *The Tripartite Approach to the Resettlement and Integration of Rural Refugees in Tanzania*. 76 pp. 1984. SEK 45,-. ISBN 91-7106-222-X

72. Kameir, El-Wathig & I. Kursany, *Corruption as a "Fifth" Factor of Production in the Sudan*. 33 pp. 1985. SEK 45,-. ISBN 91-7106-223-8

73. Davies, Robert, *South African Strategy Towards Mozambique in the Post-Nkomati Period. A Critical Analysis of Effects and Implications.* 71 pp. 1985. SEK 45,-. ISBN 91-7106-238-6

74. Bhagavan, M.R. *The Energy Sector in SADCC Countries. Policies, Priorities and Options in the Context of the African Crisis.* 41 pp. 1985. SEK 45,-. ISBN 91-7106-240-8

75. Bhagavan, M.R. *Angola's Political Economy 1975–1985.* 89 pp. 1986. SEK 45,-. ISBN 91-7106-248-3

76. Östberg, Wilhelm, *The Kondoa Transformation. Coming to Ggrips with Soil Erosion in Central Tanzania.* 99 pp. 1986. ISBN 91-7106-251-3 (OUT OF PRINT)

77. Fadahunsi, Akin, *The Development Process and Technology. A Case for a Resources Based Development Strategy in Nigeria.* 41 pp. 1986. SEK 45,-. ISBN 91-7106-265-3

78. Suliman, Hassan Sayed, *The Nationalist Move ments in the Maghrib. A Comparative Approach.* 87 pp. 1987. SEK 45,-. ISBN 91-7106-266-1

79. Saasa, Oliver S., *Zambia's Policies towards Foreign Investment. The Case of the Mining and Non-Mining Sectors.* 65 pp. 1987. SEK 45,-. ISBN 91-7106-271-8

80. Andræ, Gunilla & Björn Beckman, *Industry Goes Farming. The Nigerian Raw Material Crisis and the Case of Textiles and Cotton.* 68 pp. 1987. SEK 50,-. ISBN 91-7106-273-4

81. Lopes, Carlos & Lars Rudebeck, *The Socialist Ideal in Africa. A Debate.* 27 pp. 1988. SEK 45,-. ISBN 91-7106-280-7

82. Hermele, Kenneth, *Land Struggles and Social Differentiation in Southern Mozambique. A Case Study of Chokwe, Limpopo 1950–1987.* 64 pp. 1988. SEK 50,- ISBN 91-7106-282-3

83. Smith, Charles David, *Did Colonialism Capture the Peasantry? A Case Study of the Kagera District, Tanza nia.* 34 pp. 1989. SEK 45,-. ISBN 91-7106-289-0

84. Hedlund, S. & M. Lundahl, *Ideology as a Deter minant of Economic Systems: Nyerere and Ujamaa in Tanzania.* 54 pp. 1989. SEK 50,-. ISBN 91-7106-291-2

85. Lindskog, Per & Jan Lundqvist, *Why Poor Children Stay Sick. The Human Ecology of Child Health and Welfare in Rural Malawi.* 111 pp. 1989. SEK 60,-. ISBN 91-7106-284-X

86. Holmén, Hans, *State, Cooperatives and Develop ment in Africa.* 87 pp. 1990. SEK 60,-. ISBN 91-7106-300-5

87. Zetterqvist, Jenny, *Refugees in Botswana in the Light of International Law.* 83 pp. 1990. SEK 60,-. ISBN 91-7106-304-8

88. Rwelamira, Medard, *Refugees in a Chess Game: Reflections on Botswana, Lesotho and Swaziland Refugee Policies.* 63 pp. 1990. SEK 60,-. ISBN 91-7106-306-4

89. Gefu, Jerome O., *Pastoralist Perspectives in Nigeria. The Fulbe of Udubo Grazing Reserve.* 106 pp. 1992. SEK 60,-. ISBN 91-7106-324-2

90. Heino, Timo-Erki, *Politics on Paper. Finland's South Africa Policy 1945–1991.* 121 pp. 1992. SEK 60,-. ISBN 91-7106-326-9

91. Eriksson, Gun, *Peasant Response to Price Incentives in Tanzania. A Theoretical and Empirical Investigation.* 84 pp. 1993. SEK 60,- . ISBN 91-7106-334-X

92. Chachage, C.S.L., Magnus Ericsson & Peter Gibbon, *Mining and Structural Adjustment. Studies on Zimbabwe and Tanzania.* 107 pp. 1993. SEK 60,-. ISBN 91-7106-340-4

93. Neocosmos, Michael, *The Agrarian Question in Southern Africa and "Accumulation from Below". Economics and Politics in the Struggle for Democracy.* 79 pp. 1993. SEK 60,-. ISBN 91-7106-342-0

94. Vaa, Mariken, *Towards More Appropriate Technologies? Experiences from the Water and Sanitation Sector.* 91 pp. 1993. SEK 60,-. ISBN 91-7106-343-9

95. Kanyinga, Karuti, Andrew Kiondo & Per Tidemand, *The New Local Level Politics in East Africa. Studies on Uganda, Tanzania and Kenya.* 119 pp. 1994. SEK 60,-. ISBN 91-7106-348-X

96. Odén, Bertil, H. Melber, T. Sellström & C. Tapscott. *Namibia and External Resources. The Case of Swedish Development Assistance.* 122 pp. 1994. SEK 60,-. ISBN 91-7106-351-X

97. Moritz, Lena, *Trade and Industrial Policies in the New South Africa.* 61 pp. 1994. SEK 60,-. ISBN 91-7106-355-2

98. Osaghae, Eghosa E., *Structural Adjustment and Ethnicity in Nigeria.* 66 pp. 1995. SEK 60,-. ISBN 91-7106-373-0

99. Soiri, Iina, *The Radical Motherhood. Namibian Women's Independence Struggle.* 115 pp. 1996. SEK 60,-. ISBN 91-7106-380-3.

100. Rwebangira, Magdalena K., *The Legal Status of Women and Poverty in Tanzania.* 58 pp. 1996. SEK 60,-. ISBN 91-7106-391-9

101. Bijlmakers, Leon A., Mary T. Bassett & David M. Sanders, *Health and Structural Adjustment in Rural and Urban Zimbabwe.* 78 pp. 1996. SEK 60,-. ISBN 91-7106-393-5

102. Gibbon, Peter & Adebayo O. Olukoshi, *Structural Adjustment and Socio-Economic Change in Sub-Saharan Africa. Some Conceptual, Methodological and Research Issues.* 101 pp. 1996. SEK 80,-. ISBN 91-7106-397-8

103. Egwu, Samuel G., *Structural Adjustment, Agrarian Change and Rural Ethnicity in Nigeria.* 124 pp. 1998. SEK 80,-. ISBN 91-7106-426-5

104. Olukoshi, Adebayo O., *The Elusive Prince of Denmark. Structural Adjustment and the Crisis of Governance in Africa.* 59 pp. 1998. SEK 80,-. ISBN 91-7106-428-1

105. Bijlmakers, Leon A., Mary T. Bassett & David M. Sanders, *Socioeconomic Stress, Health and Child Nutritional Status in Zimbabwe at a Time of Economic Structural Adjustment. A Three Year Longitudinal Study.* 127 pp. 1998. SEK 80,-. ISBN 91-7106-434-6

106. Mupedziswa, Rodrick and Perpetua Gumbo, *Structural Adjustment and Women Informal Sector Traders in Harare, Zimbabwe.* 123 pp. 1998. SEK 80,-. ISBN 917106-435-4

107. Chiwele, D.K., P. Muyatwa-Sipula and H. Kalinda, *Private Sector Response to Agricultural Marketing Liberalisation in Zambia. A Case Study*

of Eastern Provice Maize Markets. 90 pp. SEK 80,-.
ISBN 91-7106-436-2

108. Amanor, K.S., *Global Restructuring and Land Rights in Ghana. Forest Food Chains, Timber and Rural Livelihoods.* 154 pp. 1999. SEK 80,-.
ISBN 91-7106-437-0

109. Ongile, G.A., *Gender and Agricultural Supply Responses to Structural Adjustment Programmes. A Case Study of Smallholder Tea Producers in Kericho, Kenya.* 91 pp. 1999. SEK 80,-.
ISBN 91-7106-440-0

110. Sachikonye, Lloyd M., *Restructuring or De-Industrializing? Zimbabwe's Textile and Metal Industries under Structural Adjustment.* 107 pp. 1999. SEK 100,-. ISBN 91-7106-444-3

111. Gaidzanwa, Rudo, *Voting with their Feet. Migrant Zimbabwean Nurses and Doctors in the Era of Structural Adjustment.* 84 pp. 1999.
SEK 100,-. ISBN 91-7106-445-1

112. Andersson, Per-Åke, Arne Bigsten and Håkan Persson, *Foreign Aid, Debt and Growth in Zambia.* 133 pp. 2000. SEK 100,-.
ISBN 91-7106-462-1

113. Hashim, Yahaya and Kate Meagher, *Cross-Border Trade and the Parallel Currency Market —Trade and Finance in the Context of Structural Adjustment. A Case Study from Kano, Nigeria.* 118 pp. 1999. SEK 100,-. ISBN 91-7106-449-4

114. Schlyter, Ann, *Recycled Inequalitites. Youth and gender in George compound, Zambia,* 135 pp. 1999. SEK 100,-. ISBN 91-7106-455-9

115. Kanyinga, Karuti, *Re-Distribution from Above. The Politics of Land Rights and Squatting in Coastal Kenya.* 126 pp. 2000. SEK 100,-.
ISBN 91-7106-464-8

116. Amanor, Kojo Sebastian, *Land, Labour and the Family in Southern Ghana. A Critique of Land Policy under Neo-Liberalisation.* 127 pp. 2001.
SEK 100,-. ISBN 91-7106-468-0

117. Mupedziswa, Rodreck and Perpetua Gumbo, *Women Informal Traders in Harare and the Struggle for Survival in an Environment of Economic Reforms.* 121 pp. 2001. SEK 100,-. ISBN 91-7106-469-9

118. Bigsten, Arne and Steve Kayizzi-Mugerwa, *Is Uganda an Emerging Economy? A report for the OECD project "Emerging Africa".* 105 pp. 2001.
SEK 100,-. ISBN 91-7106-470-2

119. Obi, Cyril I., *The Changing Forms of Identity Politics in Nigeria under Economic Adjustment. The Case of the Oil Minorities Movement of the Niger Delta.* 125 pp. 2001. SEK 100,-.
ISBN 91-7106-471-0